DUSK, DAWN & BEYOND

Satabdi Saha

ISBN 978-93-5610-302-3
© Satabdi Saha 2022
Published in India 2022 by Pencil

A brand of

One Point Six Technologies Pvt. Ltd.
123, Building J2, Shram Seva Premises,
Wadala Truck Terminal, Wadala (E)
Mumbai 400037, Maharashtra, INDIA
E connect@thepencilapp.com
W www.thepencilapp.com

Author biography

Satabdi Saha is a bilingual poet and author of three books. Born in Calcutta (now Kolkata) and living with neighbours from all walks of life, she gained experience mostly from observing them closely. Though spiritually inclined, she protests against injustices, and is drawn to the factors that determine human happiness. She is a humanist and voices her rage and grief at any form of exploitation or oppression, be it in the lowest domestic ambit or national and international sphere. Her condemnation of poverty, racism, colour discrimination, socio-political oppression is loud and clear. She is a romantic as well as an inveterate spiritualist. Satabdi is rooted to the earth, fascinated by the most familiar and unfamiliar, real and imaginative. Some of her stories deal with the supernatural and she has a penchant for things quirky as well as conventional. Her writings are simple and intimate. She has publications in numerous printed and online global magazines and anthologies. Satabdi has won certificates and awards for her writings. Her articles on cinema and reviews of books have been published in various online and printed magazines too. An avid reader, she is also a film enthusiast with a certificate from IFTI India.

CONTENTS

Acknowledgements

Dedicated in memory of the late Mr. Basab Bijayi Guha, my friend, philosopher, and guide.

Writer's note

Since there are more than hundred poems in this collection, I've tried to divide them into sections in order to give the impression of the themes they belong to. I don't claim to be totally successful in this venture because some may fall into more than one section / category. The reason is that the readers will be able to choose their favourite theme to start with.

SECTION-THE CRYING ZONES

THE OTHER SIDE OF DARKNESS

'VICTORY'
She pulls it on a leash
Head down, apprehending new terrors
He crawls, shamed to obeisance'
'Bark', she says, 'bark"

Mouth opens, collar hurts
'Bark, dog! 'She repeats'
He tries, but tears, not shadows
That once unsighted him, fills his eyes
Can dog cry?
Freedom sits weary on the other side of
midnight.
She laughs, drags the tether, face lighted
By scent of spoil, 'This for the President"
Cigarette on mouth, her fingers high-rise
The 'V'sign'. Jubilations all around
Other voices behind, dark and hushed
The rest crushed hard under rifle butts.

'Victory' - a click'
Capped heads, uniforms, mouth agape--
Things to have fun with in a dry state
Build pyramids, not a novelty
Yet proven records show, humiliation
Not even third degree

Could be excitingly effective
On these darkies- these infidels, these savages!
She snaps open trousers, freedom hangs its head
'Let's give them what they want'
Build pyramids
With arms, hands, scrotums, legs,
One on top of the other
Flesh on flesh, flesh on flesh.'
She pants with dark thrills
On the pile of exuding maleness. Bonfire burns,
Cups frothing, excitement passes around.
Incredible sight !
Strong men, naked, screwed up, bent
Sized-up with taunts, piled, arranged
A jigsaw puzzle - A droll.
Giggles, giggles, giggles. Capped heads roll.
Tickles between legs.
'Can't find whose feet, whose hands, whose head !'
Garbaged, naked flesh, life's spill -overs,
Inflamed putrescence,
Festered wounds sprouting
On freedom's catacomb;
On humiliation of obedience.
'Let's build more pyramids. Remember,
We the Pharaohs - undead'.

Pain shifts regularly, one to the other side
East to west to east to west.
Freeze-shots on bruises.
Years pass, ashes pile high-
On Vietnam -
Interpreting blurred divide-

The right and the wrong
Of shaded blacks from the white monotone
Of who symbolizes what !
Equations aren't muddled yet
Everyone knows-,
Who are so proud to be civilized
And who are not!

All along, the wily strumpet sleeps
Closing doors and windows.
White dreams on a white bed
'Washington' she awakes and says,
'Is coming tonight.'
She steps down, rubs her shoes hard
On the jet black door mat
And smiles.

Note: On the inhuman treatment of Iraqi prisoners-of-war
by American soldiers in Abu Gharib and other prisons.

AFGHAN SOLILOQUIES

1979

They took me out
Pushed me to the edge
Of a cliff
Gagged and tied.
That night they stormed
With war-planes
Found my hideout,
Razed my hut
And killed my sons.
Hoped to be free
But still I hear
The Soviet cannons guns--

1998

I was terrified.
Souls banging on unfortified bodies
Bowing low to religious lies
Force me kneel and pray
In obeisance
To wishes.
War declared

On kind.
They'll wage war
In another name
At another time.
Victim of the mountains, my clan
They hanged me long ago
To purge sins
Off a holy land.

2001

I'm born time and again, to die
Feel, pain of loss
Once more
What seemed to be mine.
As I lie-
My wounds imbibe
Hankerings of the dead
Spirits chained in mountains
And mysteries shed-
See my wife
Cross thresholds
Fascinating sparks on gloom
Crossing towards garden twilight-

See U.S. warplanes zoom
A flash in the sky
Next minute
Vibrations
Smother a twilight cry.

Around me shadows lengthen
In mute complaint
Against laws
Meant to be broken.
I'm silent.
Never dared learn
'Terror begets terror'
Blame none
For this.
It's Him
It's Him
I whisper.
Was it cowardice
Praying, to revoke
Once at least
The catastrophe?
The prayer was never meant to be
Unanswered.

At last I wait in line
To taste
Franchise.
Darkness underneath
Darkness outside.
I have discovered
My child
Lying still and cold

Right by my side.

The stories still continue……

SCHOOLING HIGH, IN BESLAN

Georgy, here's your ball, your car and your teddy bear.
I've put out all the lace
To cover-
There isn't any left in the house.
But I just couldn't wipe that thing off your face, my
sweetie
So scared was I of hurting you more.
Anna too, didn't.
She said, she d rather try putting inside
Vera's, favourite doll-
Couldn't see her face though-
And Eva's six-month old's matted hair
Left as it is.
I keep asking everyone, who is it next?
Who else is going?
My neighbours don't look up-

And little Katerina who comes to play
With Georgy everyday
Is looking so lovely in her white dress
(Though none can see her little hands)
That everyone has started to cry.
I keep staring at Georgy's face.
Don't know I waited days
The gunshots, screams, gay ribbons
Turned red-

And more than three hundred
Stretched out, and the rest-
I just can't remember.
Three hundred bodies lying,
Studying terror first-hand
And with them, attending class
My little Georgy!

Sweetheart, before you go
I mustn't forget the milk bottle
Anyway, you can't go to sleep hungry;
Your face pressed so tight to my breast!

No, no, no, no,-
Why can't I find the flower
Matching the red on your lips?

Note: Incident of Chechen terrorism in 2004 where more than 3oo Russians including men, women and children were killed when they tried to escape from a school in Beslan where they were held captive. Even six-month old children were not spared.

DEMENTIA

Between the drowsy smoke of oblivion and remembrance
The pampering zone of twilight looms.
A glint on the purple stream – a fade in –
And then a no more.
In the cool evenings revolutions disturb,
Turning sepia to colour – eyes wayward
Doesn't define green fields so near;
Vapourising; leaving distant blur.
Names trick; jumbled card games
But childhood rhymes tease my brain.
The swirling, surfing on rising tides,
Then floating frames of blue and green
Father's glistening whip, the dust tracks
Of cartwheels, a garden hoe, a whiff of scent
And warmth of mother's breast.

A sea of faces, a sea of faces
Undulating around –
To me – nothing.

SENILITY

It's not just writing names on walls
For everything passes out of sight into night-space
The hollow breath; a whistle only
Into feverish times
Melts like printed letters on an empty page.

Incidents are but dents in memory
Pushing into moments of fluid stretch
Along coastal shores at night
When age sits and broods at cross-roads;
When expected night-shrieks of birds
Wake up the putrid scent of flesh
Borne along waste of city lights in gathering dusk
The rolling tin cans discarded on dusty side-walks
Whisper what remains of cluttered words
Dropped ages ago or retracing footsteps
Fading into chaos in front; and the rest-
Just an empty space.

LINES ON AN ABANDONED GIRL-CHILD

Waters break.
I crack up
A cloudy sky
Discharging dust
On hot fluid;
Messages that wake up
Indifferent joys
Rolled along tubular by-lanes
Blood, eggs, bones, cells,
A concerted quest
Breathing into nothingness-,
And to disgorge secretly
On dark nights,
Dark lanes.

My cave is of full moons
Pushing out aspiring suns
Breaking dark red
In embryonic patterns; ribboned cells
Floating on turgid waters
Inside the catacomb.
Each year reminds me
Of a distant sun
Mourning a blasted womb

Scarred and scared
Of lunar births.

I scream, push against walls
In me, milk and honey
Turning to gall
Wrenching the thing off-
A shriek-
Moon slips off a contorted tree
Again.
I'll not see that face.
I'll not cry.
My breasts are mountains-
My eyes, two discs in curtains.
Don't chant verses on me.
The eclipse begins.

The night is a slithering cheat.
Does innocence throb tender-?
Cut the cackle.
Loveliness devours, disarms.
Wrap her.
Unsheathe urges, hard steel, razor sharp.
Discard on city lanes.
Stray dogs watch over
Ragged dolls in drains-

In dreams they come and go
Hiding sins
We choose not to know.

LAST THOUGHTS OF A DYING PROSTITUTE

Winter has been kind to me.
The mist settled at last.
Two scratched discs
Watched mysteries of night hauled out, now in cover.
Sixty years--. Bottled fire
Poured down blackened holes-
Lees of lust cemented; the smell
Escapes in quiet spurts.
Calm closure of cap.
Unlike last groans of salvation-seekers!
Sly hypocrites!
But ends; so ordinary. Flowers,
Prescribed sympathies, oblivion.
Glad I don't see pictures of gods.
Don't want crowds.
Trampled footprints
On yesterday's rib-cage
Oppress me.
This winter is best.
None but the cat-
A trail of blood
Lining slashed veins
Of battered past
That runs amok

Grey loins
Of my grisly courtyard
Now under
Yellow leaves and mud
Burying sins
Of an insouciant world.

DAUGHTER

In the courtyard trees don't flower,
Smoke rises from the one-room hut.
Footprints for school scamper
Through corridors of wishful thoughts
To lanes of lost tomorrows.
Orders pile high on plates
I wet with tears, dry with sighs.
Sun laughs in shameless white.
They come, glistening with moist
Of her warm smiles.
I slink in a corner, where the sun
Can't play pranks with me.
Cobwebs hang; I see zigzag cracks
On the floor.
My ribbons don't flutter in the breeze.
I think only of stormy rains
And mud that collects on the floor when the water recedes
Leaving ugly marks on the door.
I climb a tree as quickly
But mangoes are few and rare to me.
Foam of love floats, dancing on soups and fish
'Leftovers mustn't be wasted nowadays,'
She says, scraping potato for me.
Shirts cleaned, darned before time
Wind plays hide and seek
Through holes of my dress;

Mocking me. I run outside.
Meanwhile the mother duck
Sails proudly along
With her ducklings in tow.

UNFINISHED SONGS

In flaming rhetoric, my body
A prelude to a dying language
Gives up in spasms
The smell of unfinished history.
Chapters queue up in mists
Greys join hands
To define oblivion in seasons of spring
When untimely trains come
To crush the roadside pranks
On the footprints of homecoming.
On memory- maps
Spots of distant hills rise
Describing hushed voices of spectres
Searching unwritten names on killing fields.
Fingers climb truant spaces
Removed
From the weight of empty years.
Meanwhile ageing on twilight journeys on land
I still hope a cheerful bed at night.

ELEGY OF A FEMALE LABOURER

The basket; my heaven and earth.
Bricks, bricks, more bricks.
But tears don't soften shingle anyway.
Inside crazy head
Million maggots feed
On rotten cells of ignorance.
Neck hurts, heat salts
My burnt flesh; I stagger
Steadying confident world
On my back, reaching skies.
Employer ogles at me through rimless.
I trudge to and fro
Between divided destinies
Serving tea to men.
My nipples revolt
Wasted love runs down
The vomit of cityscapes.
My new- born lies hungry on the bed.
Behind, yawn brick and sand
Tongues of lust hang long
Exposing me, shameless sun.
With tipsy revelry
Endless toil stretches to night- fests.
I stifle a sob
While my other- half whips up

My screams, that echo
The terror of day.

IMPRISONMENT

When spaces shape up to barred inhalations
the night elastic, expands
to swallow a billion stars
in a breath-space of a monstrous gulp.
The day lies treacherous in oblivion
where you're blind to leaf-drips, delighting in rain- baths
or grass- gossips,
like lovers; pained by the savagery of the paternal wind
tearing them apart.
Dusk walks off alone, undecided
as to whether the clouds be pink or red, rust or grey.
The sky zeros on lonely promenades
with leafed umbrella of trees, ancient sentinels of moving
and rusting civilizations .
your lungs fill up with dust and dirt
choking; spirit breaking into millions of opaque shards
in a glass house called life;
or the debris of fine living.
I can't breathe in your presence through filters of green,
fast departing
and I know it's time to call the shots happily
when lids close on the screaming dusk
stifled by mourning.
Give what you are expected to give and never ask why.
Let your ribs guard your soul's footsteps
for it tries to flee the prison it created

and comes at a price.
Not a bird song, but account
for every lonely breathing pore or else
face thunderstorms plundering
the unprepared cushion of your heart.
So let my spirit straightwalk to you
O Lord,
for the final freedom of my breath.

MUSINGS OF A REPENTANT

In me is scattered the falling bits
of day and night.
I can comprehend why my soul is burnt ashes, gathering
on the pavement of my sullied heart
where guilty footsteps are in constant motion
reliving every act, present or past.
Misery doesn't heal the pain, hiding in wound- spaces,
walking a long stretch towards doom.
My footfalls in revered circles are only actions
habit of years clinging to my chest,
unsparing like a whiplash
not allowing me to forget,
like drops of filth in ablutions
or constant bursts of fetid boils on a smooth skin.
They never cease, leaving scars etched, relentlessly
deep on dusky skies.
My thoughts inked jet black, remind me I am not free,
not forgiven, so easily.
Even if I suck the earth's contagion, reach out to be
released, I know
it's a stranglehold of desire.
I ask how can I unlive what I have lived and still living?
But thoughts unleash their venomous seeds continuously.
There is none to save me.
No prayers, no deeds, no enlightenment for me to access.
Even the rock- walls of confinement refuse to believe my

repentant cries.
Strapped to my life's back the stones hurt.
Yet I want to bleed.
Wash with blood the feet of the one I want to reach before
I leave.

THE RAVISHED EARTH

Flowers bloom, wither and perish,
Others take their place,
Leaving no vacuum in Nature's circular pathways.
There is no soil that can hold a bud or bloom
From being torn, petal by petal
By claws of less-than-beasts, devouring,
Feasting together, a hungry pack--
On a live prey, growling- pleasure on agony
Day after day, without respite......
Then burning, tearing, whichever the easiest way,
Hiding prints of evil, leaving no trace.......
Yet on the drooling hunt night and day.
Here is a Life, less than Life, what a
Life!
Here is lust at its devilish sway......
Here is female flesh to destroy with might
Fathers, husbands, brothers, uncles.....
Child or elder, anyone with female shape
Brute force enjoying 'goods' ....
Joyous celebration of conquerors,
When law pretentious, hides itself
In this jungle called Civilization!
O Mother Earth, your loins are crushed!
Your ribs booted to dust and ashes
Yet you forgive those shameful births
Outrageous wretches ---- of your womb......!

Your, tortured, torn, snuffed- out cries of pain! ---
Unheard,
For justice has a single eye.......
So atrocities remain.
There's deafening stillness in heaven
When screams of ravished children
Are smothered along with adult cries of pain
But tears don't soften the concrete
we live in.
O Mother Earth!
You bleed and bleed and die.....
And no answers are ever given as to 'Why'!

COMPOSED IN MEMORY OF THE LUMINARIES ALL OVER THE WORLD WHO PASSED AWAY DURING THE PANDEMIC.

......it's a long paragraph of obituaries
trampling through live pages, and decimating words
of wonder and accolades that illuminated
the feats of icons and legends,
suddenly silenced before their time.
The screams of void amidst the deserted streets
and numbed voices of pain that collect
as unshed tears, inside our heart's crazy rhythms
will not dry, as we will look back
into chronicles
over and over......
even in these tumultuous hours,
with amazement that will never succumb
to time's ravenous jaws.
Like day-stones they will lead us to light, humbled
further along the path of knowledge ......and
from unbearable sorrow
to a hope of a glorious tomorrow.

A RICKSHAWPULLER'S PLEA FOR FORGIVENESS

I'm dying O lord, on handles.
Blind you are to rain and dust
Burnt soles, blood oozing guts;
Stone deaf to shaming back-giggles.
A rolling- stone, O Lord, I am
Trundling weight of a callous world.
Bent, double-timing, breathless;
To hasten destiny's call;
My sagging legs egged on
By denting clangs
Of a tin-can belly
Urging a wheeling universe!
We steal star-roof
On night-sweating footpaths
O lord! Pardon us!
You look; easy contempt smiling
From skylight high above
Yet reassured anyway;
Telling signs of sin -city
Are veneered
By dregs
Of a hectic day.

PLASTIC

Ducks can't swim, ponds are dried bowls,
No tadpoles, for frogs hide inside households.
Fields vomit dust of modernity
Leftovers from the machine we call body.
Between you and me only plastic flowers grow
We play hide and seek computed before.
Artifice has its own mountains of waste
For real mountains are always shifting plates
Seas breathless, heave in rage of storms
Choked with the dead, fish and fronds
Skeletons hang on to shipwrecks
Yesterday's ruins harbour today's mess.
We love to love the mask called love
Cardboard boxes named bedrooms
Here, there and anywhere only lust at soul's disrepair
Hearts in plastic wraps, bodies are bare
Today I love one, tomorrow's another affair.
We are running beyond distances
Racing fast and wild to reach a quick end.
No pristine seas, or mountains are left
Healing winds don't gladly blow,
We've built a hollow world with lies'   top show
Active veneers of hate and greed,
Where many are armed to destroy
But none to plant a seed.

IF

How much gold does faith need
To decorate the abodes of Gods?
How much money for pope's upkeep
Or chosen priests' luxurious toil?
I hear stabbing sounds of hungry cries
Starving mothers whose breasts have run dry
Empty vessels lined
With begging old and child
Or on hot, wild wastelands
Skeleton babes, preys of vultures and kites!
Outside a balloon- decked sweet shop,
Sleeps a child, marking the face of destiny
With tears, corroding innocence
And pale, famished lines,
The city's ragged interference, blighting lighted scenes
On festive roads, of a million-decor
That's what matters --- top shows
Not slaughters of pretty sights.

Where is darkness hidden? Where?
Certainly not inside half- constructs
Where masons fend off intruders
Looking for a hole to bury a chilly night!
Yet I have seen idols and stones bathed
From pitchers full of milk and honey
Gifts aplenty, jewels, gem-studded clothes.....

Seen culinary stratagems pleasing
the moneyed -----
Wasted food that could silence each day---
A Million Screeching Bellies!
Does Nature really want back
Things given to her progeny ?
How many temples, mosques, churches,
And gold embroidered Vatican were made
Sliced from poor men's needs ---
How much hunger, suffering and disease
Would these riches have eased !
Does divinity accept these recycled bribes
When haves make have -nots
Fall at their feet and cry ?
People climbing silver rungs,
Golden men with discerning minds,
In plush bedrooms, palaces or sky- brooms
Can they count the 'homeless burnt'
In flaming summer time
Or half-nakeds on chilling streets?
Not their fault. How can they guess
When holidaying in Personal retreats?
What's the cost of pope's 'humble' raiment,
Or the chief priests' chains of gold
Why diamond shops are always full
And restaurants overload?
We know those people who are busy,
Making white inroads
Into the darkest colour that lurks inside
Their Hidden pockets of gold.
On the other side, the hapless groundlings
Hide in fear of encroachment

On public footpaths
Or search for Food in waste- bins,
With dogs and sores.
Where is darkness?
No, not at night.
For even the hungry fall asleep
To forget the Fight to Survive.
O World! Count all your useless treasures
Add all of them together
And you'll find no hungry Jesus
Diseased, naked, unsheltered---
But here lies the Darkness, strong and wide - eyed.
So is this a Dream only; only a dream
Of the WORLD coming TOGETHER
In WE ARE ALL ONE scheme?

THE 'CIVILIZED' WORLD!

I've buried civilized history's remains
Where illusion of colours leads to the hunted,
To the ruthless display of brute strength,
To murder......
The right to breathe
By those supposed to protect.

In the context of progress
There is no paradigm delineating its significance
When lost, tortured souls mud- mixed, stare at me
Seeking justice.
I tread over them and with every step
View the centre stage.
Divides. Advance. Amenities. Hatred.
Colours- black, brown; creed, class religion, race
Power over poverty, values of centuries
Erased.
We live within organized gadgetry
Devoid of introspection, claiming to be better
Than other exhausted lives discarded behind
A bubble of self- devised oblivion, a comfort zone
Where humanity seems to disrupt The stream of progress.
Do we seek this kind of world,
Darkened by prejudice
Where colour or race determines Life to be lived
Where tortured, decimated souls

With eyes wide open, are buried
Under 'civilized' society's high-rise !
The meaning changes.
Does progress denote power- exercise,
Take away, never give
Make sure to snatch freedom of the weak
Thieves stealing the right to live?

(In memory of George Floyd)

WOMAN

Your fiery whiplash of stringed words,
aimed at demeaning me,
can't scald the firmly stemmed will,
nor ash that rose, blooming each day,
fed inside, with light and rains,
thorn-shielded.
My raging flame dissolves your iced rock
daring to force deeply dark, to shred petals,
reducing it to shivers,
like cold waters in winter nights.
Ego- tyrannies fail to press
on wishes, steeled by oppression,
even though my mud house collapses and I'm up,
to necking high waters.
My hollow nourishes flesh, to be breasted,
even patriarchy, at its crudest.
Abandoned, you could've died hungry ......
puny, vulnerable baby!
Even if I know what you'd be
Kindness is the natural me.
But don't talk of love
only lust or procreation.
Tender mask often hides an innate sadist.
Yet love, my strongest weakness, still flunks me.
Tricks don't play always.
Genuine feelings burgeon,

both sides,
or children.
So I sweet- shackle myself. Enslaved. Happy slavery.
Often forever enslaved even if yours ebb.
Yet, torture, suppression, denials.
Oppression races and has been for centuries.
Fear Factor.
You know
I was and am more than even
with you.
I, the Archetypal Woman!
Race me, but you cannot attain,
a mother's joy in a birthing pain.

THE DAY RED

Oh colours! Day of colours!
Waiting of pale green veins, defines a red leaf
The Brussels Page ---this time, and time again
And mops to stop the overflowing!
Add white, but snow-thaw and so water added
Because it's the day of colours---
Day of red and burning.
Dates are blackened numbers
Various scarlets, hide, not far off
But inside, terror of breathing crimsons.
Greys are inextricable, skirts, torn socks,
And those that envelope, rise out
Of smoke fires in yellow-swallow guns
And then suddenly, freeze -shots, shoes,
A hand or two; shirts brightly hued---
Pores dripping gay, then gathered angry pools
Of solid suns, in silenced refrain.
Colouring of clean swept roads with charred hands.
The day of coloured shambles, the day of red rubble,
The day of burnt lands.

TERRORIST ATTACK ON BRUSSELS- 22ND MARCH 2016

THE TERROR OF PAIN

The pall of smoke stifles me.
The sky speaks in terms
Of oblivion, while stars
Shed glossy skins in mourning
Wearing shadows that loom above--
While The Tower exposes
Malignant heat of searing screams
Of babies; and the painting in Louvre
Describes---'The Massacre of Innocents'.
Glows emanate from torches
As men in helmets briskly shift
Boots, between dead and undead
Picking up remnants of lost anticipations
Voices that no longer speak of tomorrows.
The sun and moon have rolled together
In abysmal darkness-----
Hiding amidst piles of silence,
While I look for some remembrance
Guzzled by monstrosity.
I trip and fall, the world circles---
Inside circumscribed interspaces
Of wound and pain--- a breath and a void.
The clustered cries amidst the frozen
Deserts of intense agony-I tread on
Again and again----
Bits of little faces, stilled in joy---

Torn shirts, skirts of bloodied rage
Meaninglessness, ungodly---
Spiced with malice of cowardice,
In motion of destruction.
There are no more tears to shed.
The cold core has turned to stone
As one understands no reason---
But again and again----
Expecting---
Onslaughts-----
And the terror
Of pain.

UNANSWERED

Nights are tossed around with haunting shots
As the earth's flesh is ripped off,
Festered wounds of days and years collect,
Reaching even the soft mesh of babies' heads
As laughter burns to tears.
I try forgetting uncountable horrors
Till I l lose my mind, in stitching up memories
Of flowery frocks and little shirts
Trying not to dissolve in slate -grey
And figure out gains from loss.
Nature too angrily throws up
No more surprises, tempest, quakes or forest fires-
And in between charred bodies
Or blood snaked streets and little Body parts, scattered on
uneven battlefields.
There is fire, there is smoke,
A conundrum- holy or unsanctified
Whether temples, mosques or coffee shops
Whether violent roads or innocent streets
Fires stoked to blast or roast beef in feasts?
Yet I don't know why ashes choke winds
My mind stifled with greenish red
Thoughts changing to messy puzzles
Of 'why?' Is it sunrise or sunset
The colour soft red on moistened skies
Like the form of bleeding goodbyes?

THE MARBLE GODDESS

She laughs silently when he bows.
His eyes brighten begging hopefully,
Touching her feet with abject submission.
No shame in prostrating before a marble Goddess
Who has immense power to gift anything.
Everyone does, eyes lowered, avoiding 'male gaze.'
Outside, his free, lusty eyes sponge off soft openings--
Necks, breasts, arms, legs, buttocks .....
Partially dressed, piece by piece.....
Meaty platters, served with imagined sauces
For the eternally ravenous to devour.

He raises glass, fashioned to fit the trend
Of not being considered a chauvinist
With friends cheering, 'To Women's Day!'
He is of course a faithful husband.
Drunk to heels to celebrate
The glory of the female....
His old woman's meds are forgotten
As he engages only in marital rights
On demand, forcing himself on the reluctant wife
Then dismisses her like an old, torn blanket.
Job done, he snores with bliss of morality.

Next day he repeats devoutly in the prayer hall,
'O Goddess haven't you heard my call?'

WHERE IS SOCIETY

I don't want, but see more of darkness
Than of sun....
A bent old woman with a begging
bowl
Under festive laughter and fun
A tasteless scene, a blot, an eyesore,
And then comes the nightmarish picture
Famous globally; of a baby skeleton,
Eyed by a predatory bird, biding time
Which Carter photographed,
Then agonised, committed suicide.

There are more.
I read about a pregnant woman, raped
And the tearing off- the unborn child,
Both set to fire.

Are we, digitally speaking, a global society?
Now, the worst is over.
I mean, the gruesome details.
Do they answer the question above?
Never fret, but see for yourself, a study in contrast.
Here are the works of creators.

Shanties grow alongside skyscrapers.
Some upwards, others, earth's expanded leftovers.
Some drunk, helped inside elevators

Others downwards, beat up wives
Before fornication is over.

Things often taste really bitter.
Pedophiles prowl,
On buses ,fields, inside homes,
Rape and murder, the unspared old--

Fighter pilots, soldiers, Nobel winners,
Ordinary women who have carved out
Their lives in their own way
With or without hurdles,
But cruel truth is, male chauvinism
Still exists, specially where illiteracy is in sway
What drollery, even men worship goddesses!

What is environment when you see a six- year old
Lose childhood in labour for food
Or many who are denied medicines
Die much before their adulthood?

What is social bond when holidays are uninvited
You visit only to interrupt Netflix series or porn views,
Or dating schedules and dining-out queues ?
Cold courtesies greet, and children are unintroduced.
Ignorance about close threads of relationships
Could breed incestuous follow-ons!

Playgrounds are vanishing.
Children, the future machines feed on virtual reality,
Obsessed with smart phones and computers
With rich parents providing
Every new demand to facilitate upwards

Rat- racing career graphs.
Where are the grandparents, where is the warmth
Of affectionate spaces?
Whom to run to, when trouble chases?
Call numbers, helplines, but who would repair
A soul, torn to bits and pieces?
Old homes are good for old people.
No time to care for parents, useless dotage.
Shell a little money, and arrange a monthly visit.
Duty done, you focus on your own benefits.
You're all upper-rung civilized mortals
Poor that starve or unsheltered olds
Are the only anti-socials.

It's wrong to say social environment
is unchanged
Or racism is at large with fangs of poison.
The world is on your palm; so very close
Brotherhood welcomes with open arms.
Yet millions are killed,
Terrorism still holds on.

The fair- skinned, once colonial masters
Shake hands now with the once- colonised,
Marry into coloureds, who get fine jobs,
Though some are poorest, it's true,
But shanties breed hungry rebels!
Well these are matters easy to subdue.
A few casualties and a few bullets Tame the rotten ones
too!
Society is now global, thanks to media.
Chatting is easier, Facebook and WhatsApp
Perform in an eye- blinking second

The act of socializing.
It increases friends by thousands
In lieu of a little of the warmth ....
Like putting a reassuring hand when one's low
Or joys of long awaited family meets,
A real touch of the hand,
And a pat on the back saying hello!

We live in a digital society,
Push buttons on keyboard and choose or refuse.
No lasting friendship or love --
For love is made quick and fast to go
If one is over, a readymade second Is right at your elbow .
Such relief, therefore, no broken hearts
Or sorrowful romance.

Where is society now, I question.
Bonds are fragile.
I seem to be pessimistic, else I fail to understand.

Perhaps social environment
Is just like a river.
If one shore breaks,
The other grows bigger.

THE CURSED LAND

Stones with heated hearts
Fiercely reddened by blasting sun
Steeled network of iron minds
Where stones abound; smash
Softer zones, while vengeance burns.
No greens, but smoking, jostling cars,
Honking sweat-streets, sticking raw,
Burnt tar with shoes, lost in the run.

The ground stammers obscene rumbles
Ripping and unzipping fears; skyscrapers
Trembling in the mighty swell of tears,
Crashes heard, bridges collapse
Wounds, hurts and death-smells untraced
The cacophony of unreachable ends,
It's impotence, sketches bloody; hairline
Distances -- victims and predators.
Leafy boughs felled, resisting
In the vortex, life's tortuous sojourn
That defines hatred in politics of power.

None thinks of greed's backlash
No light- tailed tadpoles or fish in ponds
Gone, cackling geese, looking around
For a hole, lonely swings swinging in hope

But lies roam freely, in abandoned parks
Of reminiscences, lost in time.
But, 'drums of destiny 'will start a different
Beat, in this comatose land.

FIVE SENSES AND A SLEAZY MAN

Don't flirt with my sight.
It may rip you apart or shut you down.
Borrowed from the brown flesh of trees
My eyes can dig hard underneath
To the vacuum in your heart's cellar
Like a good dream changed into nightmare.
So beware!

Your brain churns out reels of designed words
But they reach my ears, like a whirring menace
Of the black spider's spinning trap
Trying to catch me unawares---
But I can hear falsettos of your voice
Hundred miles away---loud and clear
So beware!

Put your hand away. No shakes for me,
For they bypass the open streets of my soul
Creeping, slithering, cold- moist fingers,
Trying to visit furry alleys of torrid zones --
But you don't know I can touch to blast
Leaving you scorched to the bone
By the skin you crave to tear!
So beware!

Flowers will do for me.
Don't boast of fake perfumes.

Beneath the scented layers
I can smell rottenness,
Every place you go
A hundred miles anywhere!
Like the princess who couldn't sleep
On softest mattresses
Just because of a hair!
So beware!

Stop. Don't post love on my lips.
I relish deadly insects like you
Or better still, spew poison like a snake.
I tongue on hemlock or lick the juice of yew
And never die.
So don't laugh if you care.
For I am lady Lucifer
And will kill
 if you dare!
So beware!

SLAUGHTER WITH WORDS

I live.
A turtle--
Ducking under waves
Swirling in your voice
Sinking, rising on levels
Of your word-choice
Irony, banter, threats, reprimands.
Scared, I carry the burden ---
Shelled patriarchy,
On my back ,
Always in expectation of demands,
Struggling, to get on shore
But pushed back under
Again and again
Echoes conniving
With winds and storms
In lashing word-waves
Leaving me numb.

I try lifting my head
To whisper a moon
Of tenderness
But it's a cracked mirror
Fractured with threats
Bars of ribbed clouds
Slicing its chest

Or a taunting lid
On dream-cells.

You holed me in
A tombstone of worded grave
Barking commands----
From uncharted beginnings
Though together we made
Life........
Yet it was only, only

Man against Woman
Nothing more.

DEATH OF A TALENT

.... sweeping the dust off darkness
she wondered where she was headed
until a torch defined a face.
Beneath the veneer of carpeted silver
in a shroud of blackness, raged the wind
so subtle that she didn't recognize
the fierce hissing lurking inside....
ballooning her burden of fear, she carried within,
cracking her apart.
For she was full of dying sparks
in her head; she never intended to bury
but re-ignite to a flaming bonfire!
Like a snake the breeze charmed her gradually,
smothering those lights tenderly, relentlessly,
till they congealed into a corpse in her brain.
She breathed air but it was timed out
and didn't rise.
It clung tenaciously to the cage
but only the bones echoed, hollow.
She shouldered the coffin, trudging
towards the edge of life.
Perhaps, she thought, one day it will resurrect
on its own.....

when she'll be free of that shell---
called love.

SYRIA

We could give you oceans
To quench your thirst
But that would be a bad buy
For you're already drowned
In bloodshed, for new highs
Of flesh; in the act of tearing yourself apart.
Will you in the devouring process
Favour the tiniest hands they can't
Even raise, nor understand your paws?
Helpless imbeciles, too daft
To fathom the politics of war,
Though softest flesh is tastier for sure,
But bony, and not as wholesome
To delight your jaws.
You feel irritable with their cries
More so; for these pests stare
Or smile, when their turn comes to die.
So what do you do with adults alive?
You shouldn't be worried at all.
For they are the ones, really afraid of death.
Others have no chance to be scared
Thank goodness, the bombs are there.
Many flee the country, wounded or in pain
But there are shacks by the roadside,
For hospitals are full; hard to get in.
Definitely they will be destroyed --

Bleeding wounds, rain and wind.
Years pass this way, the load becomes light,
Conscience is a myth, so you can
Go on warring; without end.

SECTION : EARTHLY VIBRATIONS

AT THE STATION

... and afterwards I'll sit, watching on a rusty bench
Colours peeling off walls
In an abandoned waiting-room.
I'll stare at time-charts in yesterday's frames,
The tickings, to cheat farewells in interspaces
Of speech and pain,
So that wind may come inside to stir the rust
Off hinges, along with the fading din of wheels
Set to usher the darkness in,
The whistle to blow, shadows to rise
For me, to begin again.

POETIC FAILURE

Each moment I sketch
Words with fire
Feeding endlessly on winds
That blow in my ribs—
From time to time.
Words, sun -drenched or rain- wet,
Rainbow colours and grey -white
Flirt on the landscape of my eyes.

I can't step out—but within myself
Watch, words take form
And run to wilderness, or chaotic storms
Stirring in my womb and in bubbling foam
Of unorganised consciousness.

I stand back, wait—
Expecting a march of words
From upper hemispheres—
Marshalled and sliced by reason
With decided logic supporting the rear.

But I, poor, weak and plain
Can't stop dancing inside—
With promptings of wind and rain.

REMAINS OF DAY

I'm digging incessantly.
The sun scorches me.
All I discover in sweat
Is nothing but the rotting garbage
Of days' flesh.
Heart steeled, my loins ache
With the burden of fever
Of generations in vortex.
I try finding a place
To plant a tree-
Working away at another hole.
But bones and powdered toil
Of millions invade-
Waking up
Soil- pasted civilizations
Counting doomsday.

THE DIVIDING LINE

In the fag
Little is left for ashes.
Leftovers in the meal of life
Turn mouldy
With perennial clock-ticks
And class-over bells.
Why this agony
At the end of the waiting line
Or intermittent cut-shorts
To describe havoc in lust,
Curtailed greed; wine-frost-
All this for crying-zone
A short dividing line
A here and a no more.

THE ALIEN

Curtains flap. The wind whistles hard
flirting with time-charts
while inside you creepers connive
how to serialize in the dark-
hollow names.
The sudden kill flattens you, knocking out
your senses, before you're ready to face
what mirrors hide.
You picture coloured fabrics in neighbours' rooms
and think of lurking bed-time shadows
in the dark, or the nearby water-pumps
vociferous with the thirst of people in glass-houses
awashed by the gurgly stream
rehearsing reasons to live,
rehearsing reasons to give.
On a nearby tree, birds break into a menacing cackle
tearing the vacuum.
Here, drips of there and then
float in flash-backs
of how your hair grew grey with trust
each a date with memory
how you cheated the clocks, to love,
how answered to knocks
plundering the calls of your heart
Yet the years winking, betrayed
nothing but the ebb-

the sketch- book of reason
circling the final countdown.

SLEEPLESS WITH TIME

The night has stepped in once again
To face me.
I watch terrified, the moments shaping,
Ticking by and by
Spreading vast over sleepless Sahara,
Each second instantly
Vanishing like a mirage
Before my tortured eyes----

Daylights metamorphose into spectres of yesterdays
Shifting weight of empty years
On the barren tracks of history.
To me they are shadows in decay,
Flimsy, pale, receding quickly,
Inside folds of time.
Brief histrionics
Unworthy to define.

I look.
Each spurt of life mirrors in a thousand eyes.
Is it really me?
Each breath, a drift towards the grizzled sea,
An old woman, ripped back and front
Ugly with sores, centuries old
Hunchbacked, with legends and folklores
Trying to sort out of life's rubble

A little word.
Love.

She is grey and worn
Soggy with the smell of escaped years
In search -
Though it would dry her, skin and bone
Forsake her, leave her screaming alone
Would you judge her?
Throw stones?

RAIN SONGS

I thought I would write a poem
But the rain so unsettling
Leaves me with season's drips inside,
Trembling buds hidden beneath
Floating flavours in the storm
When once you walked right through me
In twilight, into a journeying song.
Thoughts in the backyard
Fall as a requiem,
Wet without understanding
The nuances of a cloudy afternoon,
Or lanes of meanings I stepped on
Forgetful of interpretation
Of rain- songs.

FUTILITY

There can be no lines written
When the wind plays havoc on invitation cards.

I place unlettered lines
In scrap boxes---
And ponder on packaged words
Uttered a thousand times
On broken tracks
Of illegible heartaches.
Voice chokes and mists rise
Hopes lie stranded
On crosswords of lies--
Nights don't play pranks
Anymore.
I silence ringtones
Stare blankly
At invisible chapters on walls
Silence hugs me meanwhile
Between the wait
And the call.

DUALITY OF COLOURS

Some footnotes of life remain blank.
There are no words to resolve the conundrum.
Why incidents are etched in red, white and blue
Why colours of the sky is the same
Sometimes froth in the sea cries in red too
When bodies crimsoning blue at sunset
Break concepts of beauty in red.
The joyous birth from warm white womb-water
Stilled into a scarlet zone
Of inexplicable loss
Are sung in songs called 'blues'
While bluish white of heavens adore
A budding red, fated to be grassed Into oblivion by the
wayside.
Nothing's added to solutions
But a mix of earth and heaven Moods of colours
fluctuating, to compose
Life's unstable hue of apathy.

BREVITY

Hear the rivulets sing in concise gestures of joy
Or be deaf to that echo your heartbeats conjure.

Poetry is often diluted by rhetorical spree
Succinct expressions effectively,
Spill out the words your heart feels,
Short and simple verse will willingly run free.

When maddened by angry hurts
Prolific rants blunt the sharp- edged rage
A brief, stern look and turn of the head
Will do what you intend than lengthy tirades.

When in full command, compress your words
Order tersely but softly
And then watch satisfied, the effect,
Produced by the magic of brevity.

When grief confronts, cut down on the talks
No lengthy consolations, but
a small pat
On a sobbing back, works better
while you carve
A brief sigh on the wound of your heart.

Brevity sometimes is wiser than length
An effective strategy, when in need of strength.

THE SOURCE

It's a GRAND crossing of a kind
Diverging towards multiple roads,
But each vehicle is routed to return
From where it started-- the source.
They ply, adding variety, richness and charm
As long as these pretty cars, racing along
Don't crash into one another
Madly overtaking in the Highway rush.

Computed days, don't have respite
To look at others; themselves
In throes of angst, spite-bred terror,
Egos of possessing the best in life
Connive to destroy each obstacle That dares defy their
power.

Where is love and peace?
We look only at the feverish run
To DEPRIVE, DOMINATE, WIN
Be it money, domestic or otherwise Rivalries, political
strifes,
Ploys to terrorize with religion, colour, creed
Or threatening social divides--
Swords of hatred pierced and bleeding
To force submission or die.

Where is peace in this insane world? Where?
There is, but we fail to discover----
For PEACE resides in ourselves.
When we fully UNDERSTAND
That the Universe is WITHIN each of us and another
Know, we are all born from ONE LIGHT
Which we foolish siblings can never DIVIDE .

So let's sing together a song of sagacity
PEACE comes from LOVE and LOVE from UNITY.

THE TURN OVER

Nightly bliss

Mists clutch me when I ease out at sundown
When clouds melt into droplets, nestling on my eyelashes.
I can hear the distorted swell of sounds
Moving ahead from bedroom to outside walls,
Wishing I could stretch out and wrap the woolly night,
Plug in a bit of its flesh into my ears and quietly float
Inside the bubble of robbed time, sleeping for years.

Days unmasked

Days are like match-sticks, waiting to open fire
Shooting lies, agonies, screams, as I spy out
Terrifying schemes of daylight, the same plastering
Of the mundane, in ironed out time --
Shackles tightening, circling around,
Crowds sweating out the din of defeat
A day like a torn newspaper drenched
With the steam of gossips and blood-drains
Young bones of liquid red,
Printing headers of bullets and
smoke
Before ashing inside ovens of forgotten woes.

The skein of day unwinds as I'm knotted with it
Hawking hollow greetings, pulled into the eddy
Of routined chores or terrible delights.....
Masquerade of life's intemperate wants
Till I can't take anymore.....
The deceit of light, browning grasses,
Shopping love from remotest heart throbs,
Till I am knackered to the soul
For I am still the hobo, waiting for the world
To space out its heart a little more, for me to enter.
My inners tremble inside out ,
Afraid to hear sweetened words ,
Scared of smooth tongues, for I discover
Myself, a rag, polishing golden veneers
That hide sharp teeth, draining heart's moist beliefs...
It's no secret, each day is a frenzied drive
Along misleading highways.....
I see what I don't want to see,
Hear what I don't want to hear
Feel what I don't want to feel!

Nightly oblivion

The scales of burnt days dissolve
When darkness pervading the moist, soft clouds
Sit inside me, their on my scratched ribs
And stretching towards infinity
Till I dissolve in you....
O night! Graft on me till I grow into a pall....
Embrace me forever, shutting down
My ever vigilant eyes.

MACHINES

We live with schedules evenly cut
to prevent spill - overs
like wine - drips on glasses of russet evenings.
There is no space for wayward eyes and realms of
stretched idleness
such as a walk, even on a busy roadside.
Slots knitted closely, knife
the dangling edges of drowsy meetings,
of remembrances of things we left behind,
chartering a work- run, gone awry.
Inside tumultuous ambitions softness cannot plant silent
seeds.
On the dryness of concrete hearts
sorrow, kindness or even love, wheel breathlessly,
live on atoms of impatient seconds
digitally measured, then snapped, shut in garbage bins of
leisure hours.
Not that these feelings are useless,
but only worn as a mask, readied, well timed
with an elastic all -weather smile.

A facade of expectations.
Leisure, so rare, is also shackled,
whiplashed for power-births and gold dust ---
till scarred and scared time dies one day
with willing years vanishing, leaving in its wake

some precious things untraced inside iron cages
of our dead hearts.

These will echo historic beats
of what was once, humanity.

THE LAST CIGARETTE

It was the last cigarette in the last pack.
I sucked it in with intense vigour sometimes choking,

but mostly with pleasure.
My body absorbed unknowingly,
my mind was at leisure,
till I felt the heat on my fingers.
I realised it was the last line of the last stick,
and the last drawing- in, before I quit forever.
I tried the ultimate inhalation deeply,
to keep the drag inside myself
as long as possible,
letting the feel of the strong mist linger
inside my mouth........
before it finally ashed .

I have now relinquished, burnt
all the favourite things I had,
prepared to smoke-out myself
like the fag,
only to resurrect , a phoenix...... but
complete with everything I sorely lacked.

O MOTHER !

Her veil wafted in the breeze
scattering thoughts braided with dreams.
They fell, bloomed golden, on fertile soils
but petty men came, strewed them on dusty terrains,
mindlessly, forwarding the heat of times
to transmogrify those dreams, within buried history.
The pristine roots then shaped up
as millions of nightmares blowing all over her body.

Dried seaweeds, fishes and half- dead creatures
now reach out unwittingly
for the leaden- oil milk of her breasts
with shrivelling warmth,
of dying flowers.....
on a rotting limb .
Her breath is a stale tale of pestilence
mind and matter besieged,
by greedy oworms,
born of audacious gains......
yet ----
thousands bearing lessons
for her children
of tomorrow.

She's shrouded in black,
in throes of pain.........

showing only her pale,
woe-stricken, emaciated face.

Pour waters into her parched throat
that were born inside jagged rocks, the crystal clear
cataracts
that spewed stories
of lives lived long ago,
of love and inner peace,
of ecstasy in hardships ,
and harmony,
substituting ego.

Take her back to the days of her youth
when mountains used to sing in glory,
to the fecund Mother.....
in manifold transparent colours,
or to her very own flesh.....
weary travellers walking, rough, primitive, undulations ---
seekers, with tattered robes.... barefoot, bleeding toes,
yet undeterred by agonies,
their continued pilgrimage
to understand what's beyond everything in sight
gleaned by sages,
the way to the inward eye
meditating centuries, uncaring of comfort
leaving footprints, paths for us to follow,
written down on dry leaves
long long ago.

Her limbs are in far flung forests,
withered and dry now
where once various forms thrived

giving sustenance and receiving juices of life
in wildernesses and in ancient freedom of forefathers....
atavistic wisdom of the ages -- from stormy nights, light of
sun, starry skies and the chaste air.
Revered, worshipped, nurtured with care.

Clothe her again with what was once
her veil of delight
colours lost in mud and bricks
then will she revive,
breathing out oils
to rejuvenate.....
our pent up, fevered,
wasteful, lives .

POETRY IN TRANSLATION

Poetry throbs with intense pain or heartbreaking joys from spheres
Beyond transference; passions that only a poet's pen can withstand,
For essences of spirit and body, pounding heartbeats, rhymed, unrhymed
Stumbles through a pen which can't measure second hand,
Misty flavours of soul's exhalations or tremors of flesh.
Transcriptions alienate readers that misinterpret what matters or not
The creator's poem doubly removed, transmutes into another's.
Truth of poetic consciousness vanishes -- the unspoiled fragrance
Of mind and soul, its meanderings as it flows ----
Translations leave fake prints, the maker untraced with the made
Like the poet's inner feelings, subtleties of thoughts blended--
Forming identity, the ultimate uniqueness; translation kills them all.

EVENING IN THE CITY

The sun lends its burnt crimson
As it drips, on the heap of day's cadaver
Turning it into streetlights, indecently focusing
On open drains, where street - dogs feed and shelter
With men; or women in footpaths stretch out their legs,
Chat, bareback or look for lice in each other's hair,
And argue over rice boiling, with naked babies everywhere.

Yet the city holds balance when over-bridges
Rush by, twinkling and honking on dazzling zones,
When people pour out laughing, from multiplexes
Or restaurants, evading a small extended hand
As a scented hanky reaches the nose in utter despair.

Beneath high-rises and highways, sleep the lesser gods
Night perspires, swallowing the stinking toil-beads of hell,
While overhead, music of the tinted half swells
As the last hours of sweat, cool
The heated paths of life.
The city sleeps on balance.
One side, staring high above the stars
The other, buried deep in night soil.

NOT KNOWING

When I know that I know nothing
I know everything that needs to be known.
The unknown is just a fragrance of void
The road to nowhere; where I find
What I am looking for.
Perhaps the wind, whispering
In my ear, or the breath - count
Of each second that eludes me
Shouts out loud and clear,
That you need never know
Worldly wisdom, when wisdom
Of not knowing, becomes dear.

A PAIR OF SPECKS (A tribute to Mahatma)

A pair of specks, loincloth and stick
And the whole world still bows in reverence.
Frail hands and feet, but like a lion
In the heart of forest Gir
You taught renunciation in UNITY.
In these days of violence your absence
Is painfully sore.
Irrespective of religion, caste, creed,
From the rich to the poor, your ribs vibrate
Beyond earth's core to humanity's feet
Walking in protest, you led us to freedom.
No blood to be shed, your starved body
Armed with indomitable spirit
Prepared to confront death face to face.
No divide you said, but they did,
Cutting off the flesh of our motherland,
With loyalty turning its back
They tried settling matters,
Deciding on a rendezvous with Destiny
While you stayed on with the distressed.
From you we learnt, outcasts are
The Children of God.
You stamped it on our ignorance,
Blindness of superstition,

The word, 'Harijan'.
But we foolish mortals still fail to recognise
Fail to interpret what you really meant---
We all are God's progeny,
And the whole world is full of our siblings.

Your spirit is with us, your modest legacy survives ----
So does your humility in knowledge,
The iconic 'charkha', in ashrams, teaching,
Weaving, threading still, the colours
That celebrate our National cloth of love,
Born of UNITY in DIVERSITY.

MUSIC OF HEAVEN AND EARTH

The day winds out its lilting breath,
slowly reclining on the lap of undulating hills
eager to bosom him on its cover of dark green, like a
cushion
with the ballad of homecoming birds
inviting him to listen with restful meditation.
He's not ready yet, recalling the acid rock percussions,
echoing the staccatoed heart beats
of a maddened city,
the trebled cacophony of rushing humanity,
blazing its way out of the rude sun,
the metallic din of honking cars discordant
with symphony of the wind and earth!
The golden orb sensing the warm urgency
in the smells of dusty clouds,
steers his second movement behind them quietly,
to allow a cool cadenza of a drizzle,
releasing earthy fragrances, with dolce notes of relief
from parched tongues of nature,
the leaves waltzing to the rhythm
of breezy wetness,
with grasses dressed in gleaming robes ,
offering a hymn of thankfulness
to their Creator.
The yawning, tired nature
gets ready and ruddy

by the scarlet eyes of the drowsy sun
who retires amidst the choir
of grasshoppers and crickets,
pulling the star speckled cover over him,
making room for his moon-bride.

The sonata of night birds, ever vigilant,
creates a grand overture,
before Queen mother's appearance,
wrapping her offspring
with a coverlet of rosy blue,
gradually turning to a deep purple dissolve.
The children gurgle with glee, seeing her glowing beauty,
her starry maids singing a nocturne
while the mother coos a solo, soft and tender,
with the wind as a lute, lulling them to sleep .
The music of the earth and heaven orchestrates
a grand finale,
bringing another day to an end.

THE GRAND MASTER'S PAWNS

Don't throw a dice. Remember,
It's not serpent and ladder but a GAME of WAR.
Cunning and Strategy powered.
Needs PLANNING AHEAD, FAR AHEAD.
Still one exception I make.
I AM THE MASTER. So it's I WHO TOSS--- ALWAYS .
Sleight of hand perhaps, but WHITE or BLACK is MINE
to choose.
I break a petty rule and INITIATE.
The rest will take care of itself.
Let me BEGIN. See I've won----
No, no, no, the TOSS.

I largely depend on my FIRST move.
STRATEGISE how to WIN, based on it.

You ask why I violate standards
Why I flout rules.
Well, you see, it's just a private matter
I mean UNDERSTANDING -
ME and you. Entre nous, I say. Don't worry.
I'll teach you subtle TRICKS of the TRADE.
For this little aberration you'll be HIGHLY PAID.

GIVE and TAKE.
OBEY and BENEFIT.
Remember, push the pawns ahead.

Important for VICTORY.
Sacrifice, as much, if a necessity.
You know they can grow in power.
Curb their moves from the Opposing Side.
But move YOURS if you can defy--
And reach where POWER lies.

Pawns come handy in SELECTIONS.
They can become QUEENS too, if placed in the right
zones.
REVOLUTIONS however are to be kept in mind
Even though we SEEM to walk on squares .
Queen, knight, rook, bishop
Won't be able to save the KING!
PAWNS will be EVERYTHING!
Therefore strengthen YOUR pawns and KILL
Those on the enemy side !
And the rest is Yours for the taking.

Pawns give the MANDATE.
Discretion needed. The need to DIVIDE.
King in CHESS moves ONE square only, all sides.
Protection secured by a barricade of ROYAL lies.
All except pawns, only one
From the opposition can CHECK and MATE.
So beware of pawns on the other side.
Remember, petty men too become leaders !
But I, the MASTER SCHEMER, can make it otherwise.
I AM THE BRAIN behind.
My greatest strength, the QUEEN,
Supreme is her might and KNIGHT.
BISHOP is a potent player.

Has psychological access --- crosswise.
Can handle ILLITERATE rabble .
Throws in RELIGION and the pawns squabble.
Gives them something to fight for or against
DIVISION IS the RULE, let it remain so. BLAME is the
name of the GAME.
Immerse them in it.
Let them be OBLIVIOUS of their rights.
Move the ROOK and DEMOLISH enemy hidings.
MIX BLACKS with WHITES to create CONFUSION.
See how they FIGHT!

I will advise the powers that BE,
Which pawns would SERVE and OBEY
Which are destined to DIE.

COLOURS OF LIFE

columns of left- overs decorate the hall
in a feast of waste.
At a distant corner of a street
a child begs a morsel to taste.
Garbage bins clang as dogs fight for rotten food
and the child looks on, falling asleep, hungry
on the promenade near a sweet-street.
But there is a tree which bends protectively
over the half-naked child with tear-stained cheeks.

The burning sun slaps constantly as he cries
trailing behind his mother with a bucket on her head
the feeble little hands carry a pot too heavy
knowing there are miles ahead before neverland comes,
before starting again tomorrow.
She walks fast to reach the well, before others,

before the water turns muddy.
She's left her newborn with her ailing father
her breasts are hollow and dry.

The city sweats on its loins, shops' awnings are down,
street-tar melts, yet a man trundles
ahead, with a cart.
Above, the sun boils in rage, yet he goes on ;
ribs sticking out like hands, he licks his lips
passing a sweet- shop, jaws wide apart.

No stops till he's done his job
of earning a day's feed.

There's cheer in high-rise; from cool cars, elevators, halls,
no sweat but chilled glasses click cooling cooled bodies
spent in perfumed tubs and showers-----
raining for hours and hours, for bathing takes time
unlike a parched throat's walking miles
for a single sip of a second.

Winter fires line the streets. It's night.
A child huddles; tattered clothing
of a protecting mother tries to cover.
Sky looks down, the moon sheds drops.
The cold rips the flesh off footpaths but we've nothing to
fear.
Under roofed relief
we cuddle in cozy beds, where heat hovers near.

FOREST

I plunged deeper and deeper
Into your loins, my stick betraying
My legs, as I moved through
Tortuous steps; whispers of silence
Penetrated the darkness within me,
Sucking my half-disturbed soul
Which lay mute at your feet.
You spoke to me in a language
Of dazzling dreams and nightmares.
Arms flailing, rhythmic trance
With low and chilling laugh
Of trodden leaves, that didn't see the sun.
I smelt centuries and further back-
From creation; forgotten fires, dried leaves
And cloaks of skinned beasts.
The dark green from inside me
Emerged, and placed itself in your hands,
Where there was no light, only the sound
Of silence, harshly penetrating
In bird-calls and crunching boots.
I stood awed by your magnificence.
Steeps from where you rise
Clothe and unclothe you
With misty vapours,
And wrappers of wild flowers-
On the run, over your scarred body.

Many arms, many legs-shorn off,
Unlocking the sun which guides
Civilized men, to rape you
Again and again.

The old, old grandfathers-
Ancient branches, moss -clothed,
With telling signs of wisdom in decay
Read warnings of putrescent
History; of unfortunate plunders;
But you stand expectant
Of perennial explosions.

The canopy is so flimsy; I feel
Your emptiness merging into mine.

A bird calls, I look up and see
You staring at the tiniest blossom
I carelessly booted. Your child.
You say nothing but wait
For the world
To end.

MOUNTAIN

I watch delighted, while you play
Games with clouds and sun---
Stirring joyous childhood
Inside my ancient, dilapidated body
Forming cracks, through which the wind
Noses its way, lifting my bones
To where you belong.
On your feet trail marigold and roses
Making a clear vertical tracing of my heart,
As I sit on your lap and melt into a song.

I can't run wild amongst trees and plants
Yet my eyes in - camera
Catch-hold buzzing bees, unknown blossoms
Better remain unknown
Till they come and feast
In my uneasy days at home.

Why do you hide from my gaze
With cloudy veils, like a bride
In freaking sunshine ....
Your long hair of tinted mist, tricking me
Into habitats of scattered humanity,
Splashing colours of white, blue, auburn
Amidst the green of your cloak-
Till night star-buttons you

Like million diamonds --- regally
While pines surround your sombre soul
In dignified regions, celestial.

I stare and stare but can't reason
Why with mankind sucking your breasts
Feeding on your flesh, do you remain inert
As if oblivious of thousand strokes
Resounding inside your stricken heart,
Oblivious of plundering mortals,
Or do you hold on eternally
To divine blessings
Showered on your crown?

LIGHT IN DUSK

Dusk descends with scripts of light on its brows.
I wait for stars to bloom silvery,

praying for those souls' undignified departure,
millions of unwanted, putrefied flesh
the earth consumes each day.
What the letters of light proclaim I try to know.
No conclusions can be drawn by the world
bleeding for mercy above.
I only imagine and hope.....
benevolence after suffering.

There is beauty in darkness.
Dazzling stars and moon show us strength
of a straight road ahead

sparkling ivory in black- blue beauty,
illuminated illustration of the lights of life,
sweet, dusky refrain, for refrain holds a song
sung by love and humanity, born of pain
gifts divine, to be nourished more.
Peace and tolerance to deck our souls with.
Sometimes agony is a necessity.

Like dark green leaves on shaded trees,
the setting sun's glow-painted pages
love-lighting the homes below.

SONGS OF RAIN AND SOME SHINE

He sleeps on the pavement soundly
Roofed protective, under a leafy tree.
Festive lights shine on his tear- stained cheeks
Oblivious that not a single coin
Has graced the empty bowl
He clutches, possessively
The only treasure which is his.
Sweet- shops are full of smiling kids,
Balloon- decked, free whistle with every buy
Spiral the sharp six- year old hunger
Urging sleep to extend its palliative eyes
Only method to smother starving belly-cries.

Wasted food from a plentiful table
Fill a garbage bin, inviting curs
To fight and win delightful morsels of human- eats,
Barking off one, weak and sick ,
A crawling alien from a shanty
Trying to reach the battle zone.
Persistent, they pounce on it
Forcing with scratches to wobble
And flee, the mite, the skeleton.

Children with books rush out of school
Clutching hold of waiting parents
Safe-handled by security man

Chewing happily on goodies
On way home for a time of fun.
Nearby, a child sweeps an open garage
He is to wash five cars, shouting out service demands,
No time to waste or he'll be out-lunched.
The broom is too big for him to hold
No books, no candies, no holidays, No parents and no
home to return.

A little girl runs to and fro
Serving tea her mother makes,
To some strange men sitting
Outside on the kiosk bench
Tomorrow she's to pack and leave
To go some place where there'll be Good food and nice
clothes to wear,
Yet she didn't like those men
Nor did she want to go, but her mother said,
'I took the money, so I can't tell them, "No".'

Lying outside a hospital bench with open sores
Is an orphan crying alone
 Beds are full, patients overflow
Doctors too busy, attendants few
Only flies love to hover
With an aerial addendum in view
Same like that of an abandoned Girl-child near a drain,
Eager flies to descend once again
Once again ....,
When time comes, for the end to begin.

POETRY AND NIGHT

As night walks into my senses
with trees wearing the songs of winds
halting the day's insane run,
I unbutton the fever of my joints
and let the cool air flow inside me.
There's no distant corner I can call my own
for sounds invade like putrid smells
to empty my soul's belongings,
with crowded din ringing inside my brain
making me wear a heart outside,
a heart grown cold.
Practiced gestures and plastic smiles
reduce me to a doll, winded, in gay dresses
till stars beckon me out in the open
to shower silvery drops of nostalgia
in the interspaces of love and pain,
the breeze making room, ruffling my hair
awakening wounded rivers, sleeping deep inside my dried
discs,
offloading hurts ----
like heavy clouds, birthing a rain-relief on Sahara .

O night! You undress my longings,
my frozen throbs of passion,
the time when you voice
muted seeds of thoughts

which grow like trees
in the darkness of your lap
till they flower and become
poems of mystic wetness,
joy and prayer.

INSOUCIANCE

Drops of water from my tap
Push inside me, turn to ice,
Or when the half-eaten moon-boat
Rises on tree tops
I munch my crunchy heart;
Having nothing else to do,
As it refuses to thaw.
When the sun burns
I stay dark, inside
Avoiding the hustle
Unable to break the peace
Of my frozen nerves
And solid rose - coloured blood
Which I love to chew
Because it refuses motion of void.
When stars converse
About anomalies, I laugh
Without a sound.
For the pipes in my stomach
And throat are in a trance,
They don't scream; are tearless
Icicles that choke.
Yet I am happy; for at least
My voice is nothing.

I DON'T KNOW

Knowledge vanishes like a speck of stardust
Into the jaws of cosmic blackness, the Lethe
Surrounding future hope of ignorance .
We vanity-walk, showcasing petty bundles
Of paged matter, we complacent fools,
Don't know what wisdom lies, in thinking
I KNOW NOTHING,
A searching about, in darkness, to grow further
A millionth of an atom moving, roving, whirling
Greedily sucking whatever comes in the way of life
Making oneself a thousandth part
Of a grain of sand hidden, probing, asking
Why the rhythmic rolls of ocean waves
That confront it incessantly, never die.
But egos tower over our insignificance,
Immunising us to questions constantly birthed,
The eternal invite as to how and why.
We, ants, climb but are smothered by heavy leaves
That adorn gigantic trees of erudition,
And enlightening branches of wisdom on high.
Ask to learn is ignorance at its strongest .
Pride in paged letters, learnt mechanics to prove
Is like resting in a cuckoo's nest,
Inviting dangerous winds of meagre- knowing fall
Illusion of surfeit lies inside like death
Bounded by ego, a fool's paradise.

THE CURE

The world is almost circled
Hands creating a ring of time
To ward off a dismal progress forward
But bring back again as once it was,
Without smoke or hunger, but leisure and calm
A place to breathe freely, to give and share.
The circle grows each day
Stringing beads of empathy
Seems like a loop of wills
To find a way to restore
What we recklessly left behind.

Nature's disease ridden, not her crime
We now seek in her the answers,
Feel the pulse of time, searching blindly
To rid the curse on mankind.
That pristine living, love and peace and
humanity,
Can only create what we are battling for,
So hands are together held, the search united,
One world, one aim, one mission, to follow
None knows but it's what Nature always thought ....
Tireless help to each other,
We the offspring of this earth
No identity otherwise, just brothers and sisters
This is the magic cure, the potion we seek

Will be soon found
Enemy of hate and division
Nature will retrieve her lost smile again.

Unity battles disease, hope is strong
And solutions found, not before long.

SPACE

The heavy mattress unrolls after years
The caged firebird now flies with the sun,
I had kept my wine- eyes bottled
And soul mute; packaged and dumped,
Tied down with your commandeering possessiveness,
Claustrophobic, boxed-in, routine
All I could imagine was remains of landscape in mist
And clouded sun
Circling jungles of unworded songs
Cribbed, but silently washed inside by cataracts ----
I was singing a swan song.

But suddenly freedom peeped
Like a half unwrapped chocolate spaced for a bite
I munched; each bit making me drool for more
Nature called, and lost childhood friends
I at last began the journey to wild youth
This ancient confident train passing through,
Blue mountains, laughing grasslands,
Passing through freewheeling ecstasy,
With none to erase the spaces
Beginning a chapter of no return.

LETTERS INKED

She felt the teardrops on her cheeks
When he came to visit her.
He patted the frail hands saying
That he emailed her regularly.
She asked, 'Where is the pen I gifted you?'
'It isn't much of a use now', he replied,
For he always typed.
She stroked his balding head saying,
She preserved his courtship letters still,
Inside the silver box, he once gave her.
' Forty years ago when we first met,
You wrote your first love letter with a pen.
I loved it so much !
And still do, but then...'
He replied that there wasn't any time
To write with paper and pen.
'When you left me here, I missed the scented
Paper and envelopes, those fragrant
Rendezvous of our youth.
The dots in the "i"s and rounded "b"s,
Each letter brought you to me. When you were away, they
fed
My hungry heart, with the feel of your nearness,
I could see ....
Your smile, and the love that oozed
Through the written words, the touch

I could hold close to me, the paper I mean...
Just as I am holding your hands now.
But how could I smell or feel you
Through the emptiness of those heartless emails you send
me ?
I know you've no time to open my envelopes .
They're all unread, I guess,
For you don't answer the questions I post.'
He blushed to hear the truth.
She smiled in pain,
'I search, desperate, for your touch,
I, whom you left, alone, in despair
In this far away hospital bed!'
Tears streaming down her wrinkled face she said,
'Darling, each letter on a page brought me
Closer to you than never before,
Even when we lived together, yes, even then.'
He raised his eyebrows.
' Now you're a renowned writer, one who only types.'
She smiled again looking into his jet black eyes,
Then caressing his fingers remarked,
'You are now a man without a pen'.
He knew what she meant .
His eyes were moist,
He knew the end.
Borrowing a paper and pen,
He wrote, 'My beloved wife, my own true love,
Even if you leave me forever
I shall never type, but always post
Some place we'll meet again
Along the deserted path of my heart
A love letter written with a pen.'

BREATHING SPACE

It's hard to move easily
Gliding between yourself and the other--
A glimpse from a cracked garden wall
To wild and unknown forests of fire.
A transition is needed--
To rest your scarred thoughts.
Perhaps a little flower in a quiet vase,
Or watching clouds writing verse
Simply on a sunset sky, blessed brushes
Painting soft greys with lighted reds
On your placid brows,
Or when silence breaks noises inside--
A time of streaming pleasure - borne thoughts
That define with conclusions,
How to face tortuous spheres-- outside.
The mundane hours with heat of cravings
Clamouring for daylight, thrusts you
Even more inwards, to the microcosmic
strifes
But in the briefest interspaces of respite
You converse with yourself alone
Breathing in ways, adjusting,
To the claims of the warring worlds.

FORGIVENESS

We will be blessed to forgive,
Those that enter through exits of lives.
Though storm- stamped consciousness
Grabs the vessels of our hearts
By people who have creased the rope-line
Of youth; when smoothed for a run,
Or closed their doors in front
Even before invites have begun --
Those we had helped lean on us,
Nurturing plants growing out of our realms
Raising sturdy thorns, sucking Kindnesses off our lungs'
air
Till they climb up and further up
Forcing us to wrench them off our necks.

Reasons are unexplained; not beyond
Regions of lost faith and distrust.

Let's forgive without adding these
To the score sheets of our lives---
When hate encounters love.
Let's forgive and never blame the game,
Let peace enter through heart's creamy terrains
Frankensteins will be conquered---
For Forgiveness is all that remains.

COMPLACENCY IN WINTER NIGHTS

Something prevents darkness to gel.
My routined thoughts tear night-threads
netting dilemmas like throes of fishes caught.
My apprehensions.
Have I got them right?
Time to think of the roadside child,
on chilly nights-- the half-naked mad woman,
mockery and feast of the dark,
then the ones, bonfire - betrayed,
cooled to solid ashes
like old cadavers of burnt days,
or even a stray dog, luckily gifted
a rag to lie on.
These ought to be thought out;
to be humanely processed, step by step
in the warmth of winter nights.
I search the sound of my pain.
Does it mix with theirs?
I don't dare to know.

Is it an hourly harakiri, carefully organised
or a ritual purgation, to ease off conscience
on the softness of a complacent night?

SOUNDS, MODERN LIFE AND THE POET

Heat and stench of noises
in life's vomit of indecencies
stifle voices of my soul
like bottled- up fragrances
unable to scent the air.
I disintegrate slowly
scattering letters on garbage
of sounds, digitised by routine
modern devices that yank off silence
till I collapse like a pack of cards
slowly built to touch spaces above.
Places, where tunes meet
with the pulse of words
expecting a poetic birth
have drowned,
all lost--in the chaotic churn
of present life .

Silence eludes me,
a hint of its tune, vanishing
just like a drop of dew
stunned by the voice of the sun.

My rage billows, ineffective ,
soon pierced by screechings

till I am defeated.
Words fly off like seeds
loosened by dry earth
craving for rain.
They roam nowhere,
floating kites lost,
whose strings are torn from spindles.
I try breathing fresh letters into verses
but they return ------

ashes from dungeons
of burnt memories.

POETRY AND AGE

It's evening in a parched life -sky
A soiled and crushed paper
Difficult to unfurl; brittle --
Dented by fingers; stained
With vapid experiences
And ideas meeting in void,
By sudden twists and turns of fate.
A page zigzagging to nowhere .
Words appear now as dregs of past tenses
Skeletons of memory- laden days
Now a mirage, of fresh springs and green hills.
I pen old broken lines; bent stragglers,
Tumbling down to pick up Diamond-dusts and rusty-edged words
Which feel like sunset of elegies
Musty-scented old tunes that tremble and die
On faded mental maps;
Merged thoughts unlocated
Breaking rhythm of verse- tides,
As words rise and die in constant bubbles,
Creating just a phrase ----
'Poetry in old age.'

A LUNAR FLIRTATION

I drown in madness
Lunar madness; when wafting breeze
Kisses my cheek and you, moon,
Make me shiver with warmth
Of syrupy silver, changing into soft shadows
With golden streaks of lights.
In the vast open, I look at you
Surrounded by million loves,
Laughing with twinklings ; igniting
Images, as though, through the broken mirrors,
Parts of yourself snuggle up
Inside my dark, undiscovered self,

Flirting with the laces, breezed
Restless on my unsullied pillow
Leaving me envious.
I endeavour to reach
The untouchable warm-cold you scatter,
Tantalizingly---but still my bed
Remains in virgin-hunger of your touch.
The trees shake hands with winds
Their wings wanding into magic silver
And I so deprived, except for my thoughts;
The blow-away distances; till I meet you,
In my insane dreams.

CITYSCAPE

It has to be good -bye.
The colours I had seen before
Fly in dust coated monotone.
In my youth I had dipped those red-pink hues
In pristine greens, the beaks knocking the windows
Till I answered their calls.
The barks rarely visited now—
Their grey bodies stand waiting the impending
Doom of centuries, gathered in glittering high-rises.
I cannot see the moon; the slatey clouds burdened
Float haltingly, not white frigates on the azure sky
But frightened of jostling towers,
 Burying the moist earth.

The lotus pond gets a befitting farewell
Tadpoles, radiant fish, snakes and water- babies
Describe stones and bricks, until my sighs grow thick
With venom of ambitious dreads. I choke –
Sandy nightmares throttle me, till I forget
To breathe –
The rain-soaked fragrance of the past.

SECTION :
OOZINGS OF
THE HEART

STRANDED

Let the rain check inside instead of heated words,
for my soil is already a ragged cloak
hiding dried skeletons of love,
burnt in alienation and goodbyes.
Blasts of hard times can only boast,
scenes of serene seaside pebbles
without the faintest shadow of a shoreline.
I try throwing them afar, but they return,
without a hollow to rest, or a dent
in the sand, for there is none,
bouncing back as on a hardened cement road
or like empty slots of spaces,
and wind-slapped pages of un-inked memoirs ,
authenticated by its own vacuity,
left for your starved eyes to feast on.
I try huddling up with the past,
but those once - lively eyes spectred,
haunt my ribbed cage,
knocking with what went before,
the untold farewells.

In turbulent times phantom days preside longest,
like loneliness with a mask on its face.

.....THEN.....

.....then.....
......and then -------let me go
        down
           (inside)
   the
     throbbing pain
of grasses............
        :
        :
   way below
  the earthly.........
      SECRETS
        of its loins
        with only SILENCE
for company................
  till dusky roots of
     LIGHT
   ------------- .....   refuse---------.

    to sink further
     ....
 into
     NOTHINGNESS
       of

    the   deepest

DARK
   (sockets) of

          TIME

              till   my

                   S.....O.....U.....L
                   -C
                       R -
                   A -
                     - C
                   K -
                       S-

o   p   e   n

              my   BONES..........

to

          Flower   Trees
               +++++++
Breathe ******** Winds*******
               pushing
   SUN   and   MOON
                     **
          Downwards

               AND THEN
REST__________________with ME
               'THERE'
     *********************.................................... forever....

SEARCHING FOR THE ESSENTIAL 'ME'

I try picking up my soul's secret waits
but rust of habits in years' races
shrouds the essential 'me'----
my galloping cravings for worldly wins
taking me further away with the whirlwind--
and myself, the glow within
to the cacophony of greedy gains
feasting on soul-fragrance
through storms of joy and pain
breathless heartbeats knocking the door
of my ribs; the waste-soil of desires
yet I try exhuming the 'other' me
a virgin amongst errors of blindness
and unwashed toils
till I spin in the vortex, colliding
with unorchestrated calls to myself
to wake up amidst the light
waiting with restless wings for the oracle
I tear me to my own side
yet with trepidation of discovery
of a torn and silent heart----- fractured terrain
the fear of the myth of 'essence'
I live in halves, with the spray
of the 'other', in my eyes.

ANOTHER DIMENSION

I spread night over me like a cover
Only to be dragged into another orb
That spawns a thousand questions.
The night restive, tries sleeping with my soul
For it knows I am an insomniac
Shuttling between love and desire
And other uncertainties, that invite
Time - out, in another reality,
With an eye for the unknown.
So, night is afraid to love sleeplessness,
Scared of those with a conscious will,
Which could arouse the meditative eye
That sees and understands 'the other',
And visions that don't occupy
The rotten flesh of earthy realism.

Sound is of silence; lonely room,
Escape, to an alien destination,
Where shadows linger, whispering
Indecipherable history of the future.
Voices never heard in daylight, walk
The fuzzy realm of illogic, awaiting

Reciprocity which I can only respond to

In dazed inaudibles, like them.

What language is it I hear, what
Melting spaces merging into one another------
Creating a new dimension, perhaps

Fourth, fifth, sixth.... I don't want to gauge
For I am only a curious traveller.
The tense wait for answers, grows
Every moment, inside my head
As night shivers for day, I try
Capturing it with a web of unreason,
For it is afraid to see what's in its wake,
Figures from the past, who come
To talk only when night palpitates in labour
Feverishly birthing opportunities
To express themselves.
I love these wandering spirits
Wanting to reach out to me
Through night- bubble, extended
When moon plays truant in flickers and shades
And the air bristles with anticipation.
I embrace night's unwillingness
Coaxing it to submission, while I watch,
Drama of another sphere
Secretly unfold.

WORDS

Some words get lost
Under passing ecstasies of time.
Meanings decay
And eloquent expressions
Are buried under weight of civilizations
Difficult for history to define.

The words you uttered once
Floated on fluid images of present
Delivered in pace, with rhythm of mutations
Like rising and falling of tides,
A sea- flux
Or the waxing moon
Or Phoenix----

It is so.
When breeze blows on new pastures
Newer words grow.
Once your words had seeds
For future trees
To topple skies
But the ones I hear now
Are only lies.

THE WAY I'LL LEAVE

Experiences as waves, spill or drain like ebb and flow
In the shore of time, or as a book
Of chapters added or discarded.....
Relationships are like spring time
Burgeoning blossoms or as fall ,
When leaves are mattressed
Or scattered by truant winds.
I'll keep on repleting or depleting memories
In paragraphs of aging years, when my thoughts
Adding white or grey or bright,
Would freeze the receding sketch of scenes
To eventually disappear
Inside hungry shadows
Of my peripheral time-lane.
In this way a structure would appear
A silhouette framed with silvery margins,
Or a smoke line wheeling past
Each milestone of fading moments,
And vanish within the empty stations
Of love and remembrance
I'll one day leave behind.

SLEEP YEARNINGS

Slowly and softly the buttery melting--
Balms on cacophony
And consciousness of void.
I left unattended spaces in soul- spreads
Now turning putrid
While all along, I yearned
To roll inside mesmerizing sleep,
Keeping away from dim, chartered streets,
Gory treats and histories of defeats
In empty legislatures.
I yearn for cosy niches, dream of warm beds
And restful nights, writhing,
Caught between days of knotted hatreds
Is it the silence, loosening strings --
The droplets iced in my soul now calling ,
Cries flooding me all over again
I try forgetting the pangs of earth ;
Underbelly kicks, pulling out
The tufts of shame in obscenities
Layers and layers, screams folded and pressed
Inside stories of lies.
Songs I once sang, are now tuneless.
I yawn, having nothing to do--
Unwinding indifferently to silenced pain
Till dawn wakes up to crimson
Zipping nightmares.

AWAY

Was this longing to see you
Kept me awake
In turbulence of pain?
I couldn't decipher---
The cause eluding me
Like a restless ocean
Looking for a famished shore --
To open its its arms in white madness
Of froth; to embrace
The marked land of words hidden
Inside the print of your voice
That I left unattended for so long,
Without a trace of impressions
On the sandscape of my mind.

TRAVELLING LIGHT

......time to dismantle
time to phase out redundancies
bit by bit....
cravings, tears, aspirations---
a burning rocket, discarding
boosters one by one
while leaving earth to fly.....
or a train, compartments
separated from engine....
alone, headed for destination
uncertain.....
fuel to be emptied before
it's readied for other entrants.

....the ecstasy of wait
at the crumbling station
looking at time-charts
dusty calendars of life
and mile posts of memories
to bypass
and travel light....
time to prepare
in the deepest silence
of a burning candle
to the end....
the last flare shines bright

to light up
the last bend.

A TRAVEL RECALLED

I step out of myself
Drenched with the sweat of summer
In these dripping monsoon days.
The yearnings walk heavy
Like expecting clouds of a coming storm.
As I recall, my soul hungry, treads back
To devour the meal of bygones.
It is like I were there long before,
Castles, ruins, magical rides, icy forms,
Greens vast, shaded yellows, nutty browns
Rushing past the windows of ancient eyes.
I meet the wind, embrace the stars,
Smell fragrance of discoveries past
The butter-melt cuckoo songs, poems
Scattered around and in between-
Laughter of young ones.

I inhale the spreading warmth
Penetrating my old ribs, setting afire
By beckons afar, burning my bones
Till I gather morsels of frozen time,
Waiting to be set to motion
Of Togetherness.

SUPERANNUATION

Snippets of memories framed indifferently
Coalesce into a montage in my brain.
Classes, tables, boards, faces
The chaotic love of twenty six years
Breathes its last.

Mornings define a delicious drowsiness
Shafts of sunlight from open windows
On the leaves in a bottle; impatient
To grow out-- make me sleep even more.

Freedom unrolls with unruffled time
Silky and long; with essences of a young girl's hair.
But standing before the mirror I see
My dreams have all gone wrong.

I can't age; never. I'm not gone.
I drink the syrupy wine of youth
Songs mellifluous still flow, vein to vein
Like honeyed warmth from my netted heart strings--
There's dancing in my ribs, as I slice my heart
And feast with tenderness, biting on dreams--
My mind aglow with prospects of mornings.

I read the moments of sixteen
In softened lyrics; wet cotton balls

Keeping my soul fresh and moist
Inside my dry bones.

The sun is yet to set on my grizzled head
So limbs are tawny and taut--maybe
Will snap like twigs in the heat of words
Yet I dote on cloudy evenings and wind -swept trees
Tear-stained letters and silly love-songs.

THOUGHTS UNWANTED AND NEMESIS

Each day unseams its limbs to clutch me
Wayward thoughts I wish to bury beneath
Oblivious scenes - wake up and I see
Daggers flashing, slashing, out of sheath.

Life's handles, paper, pens, paints, brushes
Civilized tools that live and grow with you
Create montages of nude, dirt- cold slushes
That induce agonies, not purgation carried through
Unable to erase, eternal resurrects which burn,
Spread on your lids like a fatal disease
Aiming to kill you bit by bit, never to adjourn
Never sparing, never granted a breath-ease,
Attacking unawares right in your ribcage
Blasts, shameful, flesh- holed by a putrid mind
Like filth-scratches random, on a soiled page
You try so hard to ignore, make yourself blind.

Plagues of day and night, you, a crumpled mess
Crying for release, to the relentless high
For undisguised rest ; nemesis, oh, just an atom less!
Urging glimpse of colours in a virgin sigh .

I, impatient to be confinement rid
Try with each passing air I inhale

Annihilate bars of that meshy grid
Till my frigate is calm, before I sail.

Yet the wish I know is impossible to attain
Until I'm forgiven I'll never be restful again.

WARS OF LOVE AND LETTERS

I climb in and out of moist reveries
Mentally doodling within handcuffs of time
Dissolving in slippery zones of memories,
Joys of clean white shirts,
Pure hearts, frosty sweets,
Lyrics of love and indolent winters.

The raging heat dries up the sea
I hid under, breathing inside shells of love
But now on shore, sun- lashed
I cringe, recoil, breaking to bits
By stern-mouthed letters
Yet play hide and seek with myself
In make -believes, moments now bittersweet
Re- reading hazy letters of annals,
And tying conjunctions
With end lines.

Breaking the cocoon of ages, the insect
Unformed, hovered above the valley of words
Letters disabled, limping along
With troubled verses in vain.
I can't solve puzzles in refrains.
My barred soul bared, atlast flies
But can't rest on branches of flowered lines.
I'm alone. Defeated. I cry.

Yet the relentless march of shattered voices
Call me again with my dripping soul sucked dry
By the din of worded wars.
So memories and reveries.
Meetings in twilight.
I hide behind myself
Again.

WISH

... waves of tears,
dark clouds, looming above
hands together, wishing
I could fly...
My cloak ,
of feathers
invisible,
light as air...
flying above my soul
flying beyond grief.....
flimsy anxious hearts
and I sitting beside
ebbing pulses
sensing
slow down
of crimson drops,
drying up,
once- wrinkled smiles
blankness, covering
inert discs
before the finally
closed lids
on boxes....
only survive.
No last farewells....
the loved and loving denied ...

prison choking cries,
stay indoors.
Help the young.
Forget the old,
for they've lived enough....
Time to choose
who can't reach home
anymore.
I am caged
unable to
erase flooding,
ancient waters
lower and lower drain
wanting
to caress,
suck in
all the fear
then heavy
sinking down
on wings stained
moist wipes redundant
on earth's silent,
liquid screams....
go, go....
need love,
need millions
mountains of dry rags
on wetness everywhere.
Nothing works except
joining the world
together,
a prayer

for one single pulse
can summon paradise
with gods
and angels
of light
tending tirelessly
the fevered,
huge tides of humanity
white, luminous gowns
fighting demon parasite
love retrieved
and abundant care.
Incense
of unity
goes up higher and higher
smells divine....
permeating in circles,
everywhere.

SEPARATION

It's not easy to stop breathing
When blood rushes through your heart
It's not easy to admire the night-sky
And avoid a million stars--
It's not easy to give birth
And deny the best joy on earth
It's not easy to forge a path
When forest soil bites the grass hard
It's not easy waking at dawn
And be deaf to the birds' chirp on your lawn
It's not easy when heart cries
To tell the spirit to dance on
It's not easy to only hear the tune
And miss the words of a song
It's not easy to blow out candles
When you want darkness to depart
It's not easy to bid your child adieu
When the only road you walked breaks in two.

DO YOU CARE

The eyes that hold a million stars
Can't raise a planet upstairs
You call heaven.
In silent space of your breath
Lies the end, spread out
In splendour of terror and war,
Raging, to mock you off your throne.
The one you had hurled in deep depths
Of oblivion and fiery onslaught
At last, you foolishly thought,
Resurrected a long time ago--
Only you were so complacent,
So fragile, so eerily pathetic,
Flailing arms, whilst He laughed out
Holocaust, swallowing your efforts,
Snatching a breathless void, almost apathy
A hiatus, through which your torment
The rebel incarnate, entered --
Tearing regions of hope,
Like lighted pages of history,
Reduced to blackened and shredded time.
He spiced up troubles, in the glee
Of blood -ferrying, pulling a part
Of yourself, people call religion,
Masking with it to count upwards
Of politics of power and money ,

Beating you in your own game.
Do you ever care to understand ,
This torrid zone, we humans call life?
This swirl of eternal night
Where you've cast us off without care!
Earthquakes are nothing
But laughter at your pretense
Tsunamis, only gigantic giggles
Of your enemy.
Yes, earth has forgotten you
In its rolling nightmare.
Poverty, disease, hunger, crime
Have no time for faith and love.
Keep to your paradise Lord,
While souls of thousands perish,

Parched without healing waters of kindness.
Innocence is only goods, shopped,
 To be killed in abandon
Such are children and women.
Therefore go, hug other stars and planets
Rest in peace while doomsday arrives.
Ultimate freedom comes only at midnight.

YOU WEREN'T THERE

No, you weren't there. You never are
these days.
And now inside a temple.
Where are you hiding, what from?
Is there shame on your face?
Sorry, you don't even have a face.
Only an empty space inside
A bleeding spot, spewing blood only.

Nowadays devils have a field day
Roaming around every corner of
this damned earth!
Or is there a nexus, that you allow them to do so
Inside your sanctum sanctorum !
You've changed, it's true.
You've changed your drinking preference too.
Tastier blood, enjoying the drops of innocence at your
feet!
An eight year old, who couldn't distinguish devils from
god,
And who never returned home,
Her screams went unheard,
You looked like a lid on a bottle of unconcern.
Did you enjoy them, smiling, when they unpetalled again
and again
The little flower at your feet,

With priest and man of law tending the land?
You perhaps laughed seeing them Destroy the hole they
were born from!
Then drugging and gaming on and on,
Till they killed her.

Well, face the blame then
You unstirring, looking placid, all along,

You, a slab of earth or stone!!!

Note- The incident of child gang- rape in a temple where
the priest was also involved.

BROKEN TRANCE

A piece of glass fell from a shattered window
My soul lay alone, aside
Somewhere between brown and a colourless zone
Till I descended with kisses from clouds
Knowing then that I went to touch love
But caressed the unknown
In blessed ignorance.
Meanwhile the sea called incessantly
And I woke to build sand houses for waves.

My spirit talked in rhymed blues
Far below the chant of the other spheres
As they rushed past
The trance broken.

Home. Silent screams.
Fractured glass turning to picked-up chaos.

I lifted it up, my soul re- centred,
Shaking hands with dressed fish.
The table laid. Food ready.

The dawn hardens to noon.

Beginning of the end.
Only end. Nothing more.

SECTION : LOVE

CARELESS

You dust the dreams off my shoulders
Peppering them with chips of stone.
Rusty chests creak open and the distances
Create arid pastures I had left alone.
The smiles fabricate useless jokes
Masking the irritable your lips connive
To deceive the time.

There will be a moment when washed
Walls will be riddled with scars of the past
Denting into soured fragrances
In your room; grizzled and withered
Faces, mirror the rushing
Of what's to follow soon.

I'll watch excited, my boiling interiors
Still meriting the wait, my heart
Of sand and earth lying still straight
As before, as countless stars pass by
Night- drenched visions a girl once had,
And perseverance, till she is no longer old
But metamorphosing------a child of a girl
Who no longer cares whether hearts
Are made of brick and stones, whether
A bird which flew past, grew
 On a rugged tree, beating its wings.

THE RECOGNITION

I've lost count of times
We blended in spirit in other spheres
Even before we first met here
For we'd loved and yearned before
More than many chronicled lines
Several lives in several eras untraced
But the moment we looked at each other
An inexplicable linking,
An electrifying second of knowledge,
A mutual flashpoint read,
'Yes we have burnt together, '
Our eyes looked and said .

Even if this planet tears us asunder
We'll join as bones six feet under
Our spirits will merge again after we've died
Walking eternal shores, counting the tides.

FOREST DREAMS

The evenings drop fragrance on memories,
On mists settling in languages of love,
Or half finished dreams that sleep- walk.

The lanes of unworded smiles run
Scampering into myths of yesterdays
You're eyes talking loudly then
Of rain-mixed forests
Awaking to the birds' call---,
To the tender beats of breaths,
Rousing the silence of my thoughts.

SENSATIONS

When you are away
Emptiness haunts me
Like memories of vacant dreams
Discarded on by-lanes of tomorrow.
Each moment of separation
Is an impossible rift
Between being and nothingness
And meaningless
As grains of dust
Trodden carelessly
On forgotten roads
Of history.

COMMUNICATION

Beneath evening

Tenderness stands still

Mesmerized into silence.

Shadows crowd when you leave

To join others in song.

Skies reach expectantly

Towards mellowed red

Streaked with heartaches.

You pass------

I watch vacant eyed

Rippling waters embracing sun

In a breathless stretch of atoms.

Each flicker of light

Each drift of wind

Brings you closer still

In a way

You'll never understand.

BEFORE SILENCE

Dusty leaves pasted

On the threshold of twilight

Screen pink-grey of sky.

Before evening's final gloom

Settles on scratched pages

Of my existence

Let me pass into the moment

For a sip of that purple oblivion

The bard once thirsted in melody

Before I say goodbye.

Just come my love,

Let us walk out of circled promises

Cackle of success---

Hollow screech of crows

In the animated jungle of cityscapes

To a silent drop, merging; oneness,

A single ecstatic throb

Hidden inside a bubble of time.

SNAPS OF GAPS.

.....then write a word or two
inside thirst wrinkled parchment
of my soul ;
for it's full of self-repeated lines
sucking moisture off expected responses
growing up in wait for you.
Yet mum's the word you script,
always crossing firmly, over
the gliding lights of slippery moons,
beyond winds and music of silences,
many times when our hands nearly touching--
you retaliated ; moving yours away
with an apologetic smile.
But I have learnt to eye - snap only
the minute gaps between our fingers,
storing them away, for wintry nights instead.

COLOURS

When I ink inside my soul
it discovers the dark ---
death and destruction
scarring night -visions.

When I cross brown avenues
of your eyes, recalling days together ---
it posts in letters of blue
changing soul-colours inside
from midnight black
to a golden hue.

THE SPIRIT WAITS

I try writing beneath your lips
But you check your smile.
I measure verses in your eyes
Prompting you to look aside.
Your laugh teaches me
How to hear songs of stars
But you fold back your voice
And walk, making me understand
The sound of wind blowing through trees
Tearing them apart.
Your parted hair allows me
To brush through a lane of grasses
Creating a cosmic interim of void
Or a sonic vacancy from outer space.
In that broad chest rumbles thunder and lightning
Striking explosives to burn in me
And blast me again and again
Yet I never end but delight in wallowing
In the interspaces of wound and pain
Waiting forever, for magic to begin
As the landscape of your heart
Becomes a garden of flowers
The soil in which I don't reside
Only a tombstone with no name
To show that you buried me long ago

While I waited and waited
For centuries----- Outside.

IMAGES

Our images of togetherness
Still embrace each other
Inside my scratched heart .
I try separating them
But they stubbornly refuse
Clinging and merging,
Strengthening my soul--
Hiding inside the closet
Of packed memories
To live and sing in verse.

THE ARTIST

I was just a chucked- away marble lying by the wayside.
You took me up, shaped me bit by bit
your love entering through pores on my body
hands tender, chiselling my heart
slowly and skillfully, fearful of hurt
I might receive from you.

My body grew up feeding on your passions
like a newly crafted virgin you had fallen for,
mindlessly, hopelessly,
or so I thought -----
like Pygmalion with its creation.

You made me complete with thoughts, words
and innate honesty of your feelings,
strong enough to break through my hardness
and reach my heart's core.

I became radiant outside
but your glowing love coloured my soul
even more deeply than you could realise.
It was unvoiced agony of desire
like a million stars burning out their fires
in the silence of tender nights, when willows weep the
absence of sunlight.

You were overwhelmed with your work
carefully putting me in proud display
infront of many eyes that envied your creativity
but you enjoyed every moment
when their eyes rolled on to my skin.....gloating....

Are you really Pygmalion or an artist
revelling in the bang on chemistry between skill, and
passion for creation?

REUNION

Close the book of nights.
Let our angry- hurts melt
Within lost chronicle's diverted lines
And follies lie beneath fathoms of earth's voice.

Let's walk hand in hand with naked spring,
On dried winter- leaves of ruptured time,
Crushing under our feet, elegy of distances
We once felt, mirrored in our eyes .

Let's dare show the world again
Our tenderness, mantled by the past....
Still remains; write in a bold song
Our ecstasy, a splashing cataract
in fever
Flooding the deserts of pain,
Let an oasis take shape,
With new, green beginnings....

Write another poem of dawn
Killing the bitter look of dusky bygones,
It's not dead love rising, a Phoenix in form
But the same old passion refreshed by the storm.

BARRICADES

I watch
Dusty days blooming
To night's make-up
Expecting a desired moment.

It's hard to reach someone
Whose dreams constitute
Your night images.
Steps to climb
Tortuous with fame and power.
Difficult names to be spelt
At a difficult time.

Walls rise
Yearnings choke,
Surrounded by scope of measured space--
A breathless second
Equals a stretch of sand
On expectant waters.
The reach is always far
Before you can roll inside
Sleep-dusty, dusky years
To gather
The living moment to come.

RETICENCE

Scattering aches of days spent
Idling on hopes of release
Is that what I meant
When I leaf through a treatise
On eyes you deep- set on me?
I shift aches on poetry
Browse through word-marks
Printed on days
When speeches don't ease hurts.

What do I do?
Silence too deep to unscroll
On evenings
Standing still.

THE FALL

It matters little if I'm heard or not.
Live with times, vibes float out
To unreachable spheres--
Unmapped time, when music peals off
Interspaces of thoughts,
Urging words to gather around
Dead seasons of fear
Such as the fall from your voice
So distinct--
When my screams come near.

THOUGHTS AT NIGHT

In the silent drizzle of end day
Lids of life refuse to shut down.
I count unsung ripples of tunes
And speak with wordless sounds.
Your warmth of speech, your eyes
Drown my anguish of not holding
you tight,
When you encircle my dreams
Each day, inside.
The bark of a stray dog
Shatters the glassed moments,
Just a while,
But shards of jingling delight
Join them again,
In songs we sang
In a lifetime,
Where memories begin.

THE SONGS OF RAIN

I sang to you with the voice of rain
On dry days of coconut shells on desert plains
Till slatey clouds heavily gathered
And lightning burst birthing the monsoon weather.
In those days we talked silent Through the rooftop patter
of heaven's blessings
Drenching with love inside, or splashing
Our feet on puddles by roadside.

We soaked ourselves with rain-kissed eyes
While branches necked, each with each
Under umbrellas of shining leaves
Bending low with the whispery breeze,
Fresh breathing in, lips on lips,
A monsoon trance, you and I.
The coconuts then soft, silky, sweet kernelled
Brimmed with rain-songs inside.
We took in the mesmerising earth- smell
Clammy with satiety of wetness awhile
Pervading our senses, yet ephemeral,
Like camphor when old linen is freed
To replace the rain- wet outside.

I can't shut the windows still
The wind swept flushes uninvited,
Continue to fill my ribs, sweeping me,

Feeding my arid hunger
With soggy dreams of good-bye days
Breaking the bricked up heart- wall I built
The day you fired my raining soul to ashes.

THE FINAL MEET

…….hours have grown my love
each day passes like a hair turning grey
each wrinkle crosses the face
like a much trodden road in disrepair
yet silky reams of bygones are still as they were
and will remain, protected against ailing storms
lashing our bodies, decrepit with sorrows.
Yet minds have grown defeating putrid flesh
like pulsating images of yesterday
birthing in today's obscurity.
The past lives in collaged seconds
In canvasses of pasted years
some unaligned, others in the frame
glow-green, precious, pristine----
the anxious waits, meetings in poetic domains
unaltered and timeless.
Many events are just dewdrops, leaving untraced
but our love had taken root in beginnings
before history or folklore, we rejoice
as time shrinks, holding on to what still lives
bridge to another sphere, anticipating meets
where souls merge to become one
and only one, forever.

LET ME PAINT YOU

Do let me erase the crusty white
of your darkened soul overshadowed
by grey heights of mountains....
for winter has cycled beyond unseen realms.
Yellow, pink and flowers of varied tints
spring holds sway, leave scented dimples,
while butterflies toss dapple all the way
and migrating birds flirt and flit,

glinting orange, black, brown sprays
while singing of colours all the way.
I'd wipe the unseasonal rainfall on your lids,
lending you my purplish- blue glance
to write my name on....
and the crimson- gold tint I borrowed
from dawn's freshest form.
I feel so drenched with the hue of reddish- pink,
that the dripping colour has seeped
into the paint- brush of my heart's
green- grass beginnings.
With those tints I will paint
your spirit boldly and rejuvenate
our love with romantic seasonings.

FREE SPIRITS

I begin to feel the reach
of my vacation of unbodied joy,
but know I'd never want a comeback
in this huge ball of clay,
wear skins that refuse to fit,
and be stormed by incessant
sweeps of dusty agonies,
or rare fleeting springs of mirth;

ballooning up only to descend again
in body, gasping for air.

If I were to decide my state
after ashes have blown,
it would be the unfollowing
of the karmic chart,
of two unwheeling spirits,
aliens to repeated births,
a freedom of choice to exist
on and on with you
even as two abandoned stars

pushed out of celestial orbit
to die in embers of love,
leaving forever a trail of sublimity
inside the eternal cavern of no return
indistinguishable ashes of us

unseparated, mingled forever
inside the jaws of timeless black
permeating the silver speckled
deepest blue.....

THE REACH

The fragrance of my soul is pure incense
For it's a flower of worship
Born from the womb of dreams,
A love I can't hand over to you in body.
Yet if you wish, reach out to me in ardour
Of your heart's pain, passionately

Drumming your throbs so strong
That they run to embrace --
I'll absorb through pores of my silent waits
Sounds, flooding the parched soil of my life.

WAITING FOR THE TWILIGHT

I dream and wait, my soul,
a filigreed mirror reflecting your face,
is shelved inside the echoes of my heartbeats,
and my limbs torn apart in an alien sphere
I decide cheating the world, thinking of you.
I tie my pain in anticipation,
the ecstasy of our merging spirits
soon to be played out by the cosmic fusion in twilight,
the music sensed through the third disc hidden above my
brows.

That's why my dark blood loves to be laced with gold,
loves to keep flowing softly towards the wise - sinking sun,
on waters of golden pinks and light greys
while darkness thickens the crown on my head
when whitened are on the way.

DREAMS FOR MYSELF

Just ease and let yourself settle in my dreams.
I'll never ask for more.
It's within the scope of my vision
I love to see you float each day---
Picking up the pulse
Of your entries and exits
With words gliding in and out,
To be birthed on sheets of sunlight
When poetry comes of age.

In between waves of nights and days
I swim, in darkness or in light
Of your gaze ; the letters of time, Lost in colours of ecstasy
Tides that flow
Wetting me inside.

Such are the uncharted zones--
My dreamscape, where roaming freely,
With you, deeply into my eyes,
I let ourselves play to eternity!
Many times I felt those uncaressed caresses,
Many times our lips touched words but never touched,
While I wallow in, careless of the escaping dark,
And never reaching you--- at all.

Yet I know for sure, these mental clicks
Will survive, as long as my memory is alive.

ROADSIDE BARTER

I had bartered my soul once
for a few of your dreams
which left by the roadside
redundant, you let grow.

But if I could ask
you wouldn't have given
orbs of light, like golden coins
made from the purest tint
of your heart ---
for now you know it's not me
your eyes search.

Yet I'll stick around
to gather by the roadside
the wasted parts of yourself,
your carelessness -----
for those are the things
I harvested
that hurt and cry with me.

FINGERS

The day you held my hand
It was as if the earth
Sealed its sweating lips tight
To shut off whispers in the air
That roamed beyond our fingertips.

How warm and safe the nest-
Guarding nails barricading time
As it whistled away between the chinks
With storms of years-
My throbbing fingers cushioned-
My soul stretching forward to yours
In certainties of future claims.

The day you let go, it was washed-
Your thumbs in a dance of mockery
Trembling inside my ring of tears
The forefinger dictating terms,
And the rest, erasing rural lights
Of evenings ; my palm in empty unrest
Like a page fluttering in the void
A virgin page, whose tale had not begun.

THE SAID AND UNSAID

When you unsaid what you said
It was just rocks hitting a silted shore
Smashing what I believed was bred
Between us, so many years before.

Sky fell down on jagged plains
Blood-drenching grasses grown so dense
As I juggled with my gains and my pains
To revive my lost soul to present tense.

The looks you gave once, laid out bare
With blanks, like a form for me to fill
Synonyms for love, warmth, tenderness, care
Now left rusting, sit on your windowsill,
To winds and rain, to my agonised screams
Lifting them up to see how they die....
Yet they grew, feeding on blinded dreams
And air of my long untangled sigh.

Inside moist grasses wafting in the breeze
Hide those forgiven thorns on new roses
A fragrant spread, doesn't vanish or cease
But lovelier, even though hope closes.

They climb walls, passion's vacant spaces
Fiercely restless to touch longing's height
Pulse beats challenged, winning races

Can't tame love's unrequited might.

Helpless, I recall what we together felt
Were just wounds of words I heard, misspelt.

RECONCILIATION

I can read thunderstorms.
The season's burst of moods
Such as when sparrows brood
Over mountains of mist-
Or dust sweeps through carpets of green.

Your nostrils twitch and eyelids bat
Making claims of stormy monsoons
Deep in my heart
When the wet crow shivers
Weighed down with moistened wings
That I embark-
On a dangerous journey of wind and rain.

Yet this time of year comes
In the swelling heat of mangoes
Invisible ripenings registered
On empty tracts of absence.
Soft footfalls on patient time
When buds grow hankering for form
Sweetened fires encouraging
Forgetfulness of the 'other' season.

Summer is not a myth, nor unseasonal spring
When autumn vanishes shivering
And storms at last decide

To wake sleepy oceans
With ravishing tides.

WIRELESS

From a distance I can read
the posts you send from your eyes,
the subtle void that transports your agony
through the grey of the waters of your eyes
transmuting into an urge to be by your side
when alone with you in my thoughts.
The road you're travelling is fraught with pain
and even if I wanted to,
I can't unfurl the tenderness inside,
spreading it wide over your troubles to make your journey
smooth,
for I am classed and zoned in a fake paradise
preventing me from reaching you.

I can only rely on hunches and subtle signs
to pass on soul to soul messages
to say, I am always by your side.

SECTION :
BEYOND

CONTRARY SPIRIT

Billion stars etch your name
In cosmic turbulences of surreal lights
Igniting a solitary fire in the lonely portal
Of my heart, demanding a song.
I try chanting by rote the lines forefathers set
Humbled by your terrible force.
But Om Shantih! escapes; - a nowhere
My lips voicing aspirant fears
In the horrid circle of death.

As I fold my hands in supplication.
My brain erupts in contrary madness
The pain, this fever, your radiance denies
Those microcosmic dreads inflated
Ripping the loins of the earth
To nether spheres. Yet I know your kisses –
Drops of dew on dawn-stirred trees,
Migrating birds and baby-stirring wombs;
On dry leaves on torrid zones,
But empty – bowl screech millions,
Virgin red in monster carpets , killer drones
Can't define my heart – your own.

THE UNKNOWN

I don't understand why doodles upset me.
In the still darkness of my unnamed self
I mistake figures that make meanings
In black and white; yet in spite of the insensible
Credulity of living a well-rehearsed life
The over-boundaries threaten me with thunderstorms.
On the table an unread book, a focus on the dangerous
Chapters of mist, I avoid consciously, though curtains flap
In the wind, a wake-up call, to unroll
The secret river inside
The hungry receptors of my brain.

I am careful to carry a hood, to ward off
Undisturbingly disturbing calls: yet head
To the terrace to seek out what remains sensible
Beyond the parameters of time
The criss-crossing of shadows, a burst of air,
Chills the advocacy of reason
I wait, I wait for the moment to come.

WISHFUL THINKING

Will you ever try, even in a dream,
Writing a page inside my heart,
Just like names carved on a tree,
The branched veins commuting
What you once wanted to say to me,
Or look in my eyes, just as stars see,
When rivers are lulled to sleep
At moonrise ; their faces softly mirrored
On half-lights of the moving deep?
Still if you resist, shall I, like the grassland,
With the dancing wind, sing, or bird- whistle
To the unreachable clouds, calling
Off- tune, so that the jarring sound
Strikes hard at your vacant ribs.

COME NIGHTLY, MY GOD

Come, sit by me, my God,
Once only, this desirable night.
I want to feel the moon
Locked in your cosmic smile.
It is dark and the breeze
Carries whispers of your love
In scented blooms and leaves.
I know I am the lowly grass
Bent over to clutch you tightly .
You, old, old embracing earth.

I see you laughing in stars--
Within and without, in the dark
Voiced, yet voiceless
So near me, yet so far apart.

DIVINE WHIPLASHES

I step out of myself to understand
The folly of your creativity.
Befuddled, I can't reason with that cosmic impulse
That rushed through your senses
Leading to genesis .
You roared in gusts of pristine   fires and quakes
To chart out the beginning
Of the circumambient tints of being,
Yet a fruitless and wasteful expenditure
Of the primeval heave to propagate ,
Then gradually to deconstruct bit by bit.
You, giant baby, dashing the mud-ball
Self -designed, for the infernal pleasure
Of hearing it crack and peel off.
As the bard said, it is just a sport enjoyed.
Your wild-fire laughs in ashes of greens,
Storms or waves whiplashing into pulp,
Upper crust to dregs, pushed in a bowl ;
There isn't any escaping, fated creatures,
Born of whims and hyperboles .
Your earthquakes, jaw monstrously,
Crushing, grinding, pounding with relish
Figures, minute and large--
Your signatures; kind lord, ethereal,
Defeating efforts of the bold
Eager to outsmart you in fair,daring games,

On the chessboard of life.
Your lust for command and control
Is a passing scare, yet most are still pawns
Netted, in dread of your calamitous wrath,
Subverting them to devotees
Of your super power.
Others are better employed,
To wield your banners
In religions devised, creating
War, division and despair.
Divinity unchallenged therefore.

BLINDNESS

I hired evenings from days chores
for Sunday toils,
to walk the crossways of body and spirit
rehearsing words I wished to convey.
Verses grew like trees in full bloom,
thick and fast and before I knew
I learnt them all, by heart.
I longed for you, sitting still or floating
in the darkness of my soul's illiteracy ----
yearning for you to come and open my window
to the eyes of daylight where I could see you face to face
waiting amidst years of oblivion.
Yet so foolish was I not to realise
that seeing is not finding you.
It's the scream of absence
that always defines
the force of your nearness
beating deep and wide, inside me.

A parched throat's thoughts of a drink
is a pleasure, very few recognise.

VANISHED SWEETNESS

Don't stop my walking into thoughtfulness
For going out of myself, is melting in the present
I slip and fall and the blood runs dry
With the heat of pain.
Beneath the slate -grey mantle of death
The sky in me labours for a rain-relief
Instead, it vomits only crimson in verse.

Do you call me, O lord, to see this world
And write answers to 'why', from beginning to end?
I cannot, in the windy blast of blackened time
Arrange, fold, reconstruct, lost sweetness in prayer
In the chaos of my fevered brain.

THE DIVINE MELODY OF LOVE

You play,
fingering chords that orchestrate
into desires rising and melting,
vibrating trebles and bases
all over the octaves of my body.
The staccatos send shocks, temporary--
while the sonata of soul and flesh
harmonise into holiness;
movements waltzing
into deepest sweeps of the spirit ocean.
The crescendo is the reach of bells
ringing for evening prayers---
lighted lamps, fragrance of flowers,
rising upwards like incense-swirls
till I am oblivious of corporal hemispheres
and the moment of joy metamorphoses
into a hymnal offering
of oneness
as we fuse together
in a cosmic embrace,

as children of greater gods,
you forget who I am,
and I, who you are.

I'LL KNOW YOU THEN

It's not that I see you
But you still talk in answers
Within, assigning me to keep watch
Between rise and set of the sun's motion
And count the empty drips
Of moments in blues, inside my brain.
These waits , these longings are avenues
To your presence, when sleepless,
I'm tossed around like wind on leaf
Drawing breath, a womb in pain, urgent,
Hoping to find you sitting patiently
In the density of birth aspirations
But I forget you are me
And I you, as my eyes mirror
Your muted laughs when you play
With my heart's fire,
Or within the rhythm of your silence
That pervade in blessings ----
Like perfume, to balm
My agonised soul.

BAFFLING SEASONS

You draw on blue-white canvas
With ink-dipped cotton on high
I try copying you in the feel of monsoons
But suddenly you paint a golden orb
Flashing on a grey drenched sky.
Your tricks upstairs, baffle me.
When I try working on dry leaves
You post splashes and pours
Battering my ambitious try.

Who are you and what are you
Disturbing, leading me to mundane days
And brain- rattling, restless nights?
Swoon me with your scented lies
About happiness, love, peace and no goodbyes
Your canvas so deceptive and yet am helpless
My love is too palpable
To be packaged alive.

TRAVELLING WITHIN

.....the doors are eternally open,
but we're blind.
Confinement defiles the mind.
I extend within,
see winds breaking clouds,
weaving white-grey flowers in the blue.
I float, blissful unrolling......
an ethereal stretch, limitless ,
the fire I didn't believe in
airing me like winged leaf undulating
along the middle of sky and ocean,
in an ecstasy of transcendental motion.
My flaming spirit often
is wafted by the unknown
in amazement of silent revelation
of what it is 'To Be'.
Unbodied, I am sucked into the creative vortex
my fire, guided gently
from conscious to immeasurable expanses,
to the source of the eternal 'I'
for it is myself, I discover.

I'm spirited by the boundless,
marshalled by the greatest light
of which I am always a part,

yet totally apart,
from the all pervading 'Om'.

INDIVISIBLE

They say I'm you and you me
Then where do you reside?
When in agony and ecstasy
I look for you, by my side--
I search in and out,
With storm -breaks and cloud- pass
When lambs bleat to happiness
And the country green, laughs, content
Or when the river of blood overflows
And bleeding, the earth cries in vain
I desperately try to hang on to you
Try to find echoes of your voice
Inside my tattered limbs.
But suddenly realization dawns--
I'm such a fool to divide-
Your cosmic wrapper of light
That envelops each leaf or a speck
Of dust; who was I to decide ?
A fool; for each feeling I receive
Is yours--never to be torn aside.

TESTS

You thrust me often inside a tunnel
And fill it up with coal-dust.
Then breath becomes tortuous
Like a drop of water at long intervals
In arid throats .....
And on the roof, deafening screams
Of trains shatter all hopes
Of escape, no holes to ventilate,
Till you come to my rescue, O lord!
It is then that I start digging another tunnel
Inside me --- to flee from the unbearable
Ambience of the world
You do it purposefully
So that I could walk on fire and purify
My torn spirit to freedom,
Realise you are in me......
My Sun, my Love, my Redeemer
Till it is You I finally see.

SOUL

Shedding of cloak
Then unmasking.....
Nakedness opens
Million of miles
Of walks Inside .
I discover
Endless spaces
Opening up.....
Charged with cosmic lights
A link
With the vibrating vast ;
Limitless ....

Nothing touches
Asleep or awake
No echoes ---
Of the madness
Outside .
I know that I am
Knowing Me......
Another universe
Amongst universes
A part of tremendous whirl
Unvarying process
Of eternal change
Many bodies.....

Many spheres
Many lights
But one unchanged
Consciousness......
Celestial
A luminous string.....
Yet abstract
Holding fast
Many forms
A Connect
To the ultimate Being.

THE UNIVERSE WITHIN

The night strolls beyond the pillow
Crying to reach your presence.
I wait and wait to hear the silent signatures
You leave on my bed, beside me.
I try to hold on to the essentials
That mark your nearness
Like an unseen dream.
My hands dotted with goose bumps
Become antennas trying to catch
The holiness pervading the dark;
Smells of night turning to incense
And minutest sounds to chants
When gliding in and out
Of the rhythm of my breathlessness
You pour the balm of muted music
In the whirl of universes' cycling ,
Enveloping me in oneness of which
I am a part,
Gathering my scattered identity.

PRESENCE

From the palm, rises the incense
climbing between my fingers---
a clue to your presence.
The prayers of midday surface
without fire of sticks
yet with a deep calm underneath.
It's past midnight, as I lie in wait
for you to pervade my consciousness,
gliding to a trance between this and another dimension
a birth amidst infinite layers
of the eternal conundrum
of what is and what is not.
My heart breathes in the essence
of peace and harmony
as night, after day- toil settles down
to voices in other planes; guides
who surround me everyday;
invisible to the naked eye.
Their caressing fluids slowly wash
fires of flesh, as my soul merges

into a bliss of oblivion of the Now.
My heart refuses a walk, blending inside, with my spirit,
for you take them in your hands to bless.
The cacophony is stilled, cares folded into nightshade,

a prelude to your great entry, sensed within,
you, a mirror I witness my best .

Permeating through and through,
you finger my veins, like strings of a sitar.
The musical journey vibrates
with your monumental love and pain
treble and bass
culminating to an all- embracing
hymn for earth.
You cry for us all, through soul and body,
the epiphany in my subconscious- conscious self,
that transports me back
to Now again.

A VIEW BEFORE DARKNESS AND AFTER

Before the night cover is spread out,
before hands tick to a stop inside me,
before preparing for a new journey,
I retrace the wilderness of my heart,
to view the still sadness of an ending.

The dried leaves ; the veins,
remnants of the green-shooting joys of arrival,
when I was a child,
are now silenced by groans
of the passing wind,
tired and burdened with vacancies.

I was a mere bud you tried to blossom,
appearing in many forms, but I, wet with rains,
wasn't aware of the roundness
of the tunes you played on my truant spirit ,
fingering the keys of my being so lovingly,
playing on happiness of beginnings,
which only half- opened petals never sensed
for they couldn't look beyond
the star- dusted moonlight and father's 'coming - home'
scent.

So, only resonance of initiations stayed.
When I bloomed well enough
to discover your games,
you eluded me with pranks
of passing shadows, glimpses
of gossamer wings; fanning me to dreams,
of misty flights and imagined songs.

And now when the sun cools a faded red in my veins
I am full of wounds in sounds or slaughter in words
that invade the emptiness in my drooping limbs,
to a riot of flushed crimsons,
the torrid zones----
unseasonable anger, cruelty, pain.

My soul is dissected, measured, commandeered to be
preserved
by 'holy waters' of religious freaks,
that 'operate' in wanton lust---
countless children too,
unspared, under political spotlights;
'ministered' for gains--
in deaths without cause.

Depressed , I couldn't even get through
the cosmic equivalent -------
of the infinitesimal 'I am' .

Why? And where are you?

I cry out loud for your mercy.
But the shroud is ready to cover me too.

Yet, before leaving, I say,
'It is for now only, only now'.
The price will be paid
for the blood of innocents.
The countdown begins.

There will be births
and endless beginnings of joyous things.

AUTUMNAL HYMN

My autumn - eyes suck in
Ebbing waters of rusty sunsets,

Like crimson, bathed in blue,
Tempting me to sip the mixture
Of purple, the 'winking' glass,
A junction, where spirit talks
Through dissolving flesh--
A reincarnation of life's verse
Where you melt in me or otherwise
In a drink of past tenses ; eyeing
What is to come in the feast of future.
We grow in knowledge of the fall,
Seasons of pain yet joyous,
In birth of understanding the unknown.
A season of leafy meetings though carpeted
With crunchy yellows, yet,
Speckled with oranges, reds and dark greens.

SECTION : MICRO POEMS & HAIKU

PANNING

Poems have eyes. On one side
skeletons, huts unroofed, bent over hushed up wastes,

scream- silenced lips
to concrete buildings tall, meatings,
voices cheery- loud....... the other side.

I write.....tears, laughter ......and add up
Life.

EYES

Your eyes are x- rays
probing deep inside my ribcage
But in spite of the search
you can't locate
your hiding place.

BAR

the pond, a still mirror
I wish to see me reflect
but there floats your face
my dreams swimming recklessly
striking on unbreakable glass
in front of my other self.

JOURNEY

Vapours emit from caves
Rising with elemental mergence
Formless multitudes of planes
To brief or prolonged pauses
The journey begins again
Innumerable universes
Back into a frame.

BLIND

Don't look away
For I see my blindness
In your eyes
Falling stars
At end- day.

BLANK

I live dreams
Like half-formed letters
Refusing to take shape
On an empty page.

Scattered joys

Wound-mouth opens
And fresh blood flows
Wetting my breast- pocket
Where once I hid a few joys
Lying on the roadside
Unattended.

SOLITUDE

Crowds abuzz, festive laughter
I mix madness outside
Yet my heart writes silently
A rendezvous with me.

RETURNED BROKEN

I bartered my soul with your spirit
But you returned mine back one day
Like shards of glass that cannot be joined
Yet getting back yours intact,

 the tear- filled marble grail.

CREVASSE

It's best to strap moonlight on shoe strings
It torches crevasses we overlook
While exulting in an evening sky.

ASHES

I burnt my soul
and left the ashes
at your door
as remembrance !

HAIKU-1

227

I'm not your sapling
You, huge, strong, yet so distant
I'd be an ivy.

HAIKU-2

Your golden tower
Your wines, loves, songs, laughter-- but
My withered flower.

HAIKU-3

Night, like endless shroud
Cells cannot ever pervade
Only consciousness.

HAIKU-4

I'm scared of mirrors
Seeing your mistrust burning
Deep inside my eyes.

HAIKU-5

231

Find you in silence
voice mingled with my heart's sweat
You dry, but me, wet.

HAIKU-6

In the fag of life
Ashes pile up, devouring
History with fresh lies.

HAIKU-7

233

Screech of loneliness
Invades my unpacked heartbeats
Forcing a fold back.

HAIKU-8

Final bell will ring
Keep note of what you left home
Whichever road reached.

HAIKU-9

235

You talk without stops
Like the booming waves ashore
Shutting my lips doors.

HAIKU-10

Take me or leave me
But don't ever ignore me
I'm dreams saving lives.